Copyright © 2024 ThatNickPowersGuy LLC
All rights reserved.
ISBN-13: 979-8-218-41624-9

This book represents the author's opinions and is merely a starting point for analysis. Data and interpretations within this book should be further explored and researched by those reading. Nothing in this publication, or any publication, should be taken at face value by readers without researching further on the topic or consulting an expert.

In a day and age when errors, bias, and even intentional misrepresentation of data in nonfiction books are a relatively common occurrence, it's important to fact-check what you're reading and explore information from many sources. There is no perfect book, nor is there a perfect author. Although this book was fact-checked and reviewed, and this publication is determined to be accurate, critiques are always welcome. If you find any errors, please send an email to
Contact@thatnickpowersguy.com

QUICK! VOTE... Before You

by
Nick Powers

Standard Cover Illustration Copyright © 2024 Nick Powers and Ryan Haines
All rights reserved.

For my mom:
(Michael and Matt too, I guess.)

Contrary to popular belief, the ability to be impartial, objective, and to think critically are all learned skills. When I think about my own ability to research with nuance, humility, and compassion and put all beliefs aside, all memories trace back to you.

You taught me how to learn.
So, in a way, you taught me everything I know.

Table of Contents

Introduction 1

Party Loyalty 5

Differentiating the Parties 17

Affordability of Blue vs. Red States 23

Poverty and Political Affiliation 39

Blue and Red Cities 43

Raising a Family in Red vs. Blue States 55

Funding to Democrats vs. Republicans 61

Legislation by Democrats vs. Republicans 75

Voting Third Party 93

Simulating the Odds Third-Party Candidates 116

Simulating the Odds of a Third-Party Celebrity 125

If all of us Voted for a Third-Party Candidate .. 131

Voting Third-Party in Protest 135

Eliminating the Electoral College..........139
What Can We Do?..................................141
Table of Figures.......................................145
Bibliography..151
Index 167

Introduction

Letter from the Author

Before we start, I want to clarify that this book is meant to be a quick educational resource. No matter where you stand politically, how educated you are about how our political system works, or how invested you are in learning about politics, the goal is to provide something meaningful and interesting to you. I want you to learn what you can without the pressure of digesting all of it. There may be parts of this book that aren't relevant or are uninteresting to you. If that happens, skip that part. Do it guilt-free, as though you were scrolling past a video on social media. You do not have to read this book in its entirety.

That includes this introduction.

If you're getting bored, skip ahead.

If you know something already, skip ahead.

If you see something in the table of contents and want to skip to that section, do it. Skip to that section.

However, if you're about to skip a chapter because you disagree with one of my points, my challenge for you is to read through it and challenge both your beliefs and the text in the book equally. Finish the section, look at the sources, and read additional resources. Find a way to learn something new or change your opinion.

That being said, *Quick! Before You Vote!* contains very few political opinions. Instead, it presents verified facts and data. This book was created to inspire you to challenge your own beliefs as well as those you disagree with, and hopefully, everyone can learn something from it. I certainly learned a lot from compiling all this data.

But for now, those who know me may be asking themselves why I authored this book.

Those who don't know me might ask, "Who the hell is this guy?"

In late 2021, I started making content on the internet full-time. In the span of just a few years, my channel has grown from zero to half a million followers, and my life has completely changed.

I left my tech job to pursue content creation, and while it's extremely stressful at times, I've been loving every second of it.

My followers sometimes ask why I don't publish a scholarly paper.

But... *here's the thing.* Scholarly articles aren't easily accessible to those outside of academia. Even when the articles are free or can be obtained by emailing the author, they're often difficult to read, sourced by other inaccessible articles, and... to be frank, boring.

If you show me someone who would rather read scholarly articles than scroll through TikTok, I'll show you someone who already knows enough to educate themselves.

So... no, I'd argue the opposite point. As a TikTok influencer, I'm able to share the data and resources from my research more broadly and connect with people who might not otherwise have been exposed to critical thought in politics. Publishing academic papers and teaching college-level courses feels like a waste of my research. My work is reaching people who want to learn... in three minutes or less.

There are many problems with education via short-form content. To begin, it's, well, short. I can't explain everything all in one video because the algorithm favors videos that are shorter than three minutes. Any longer than that, people are less likely watch all the way through and it doesn't get on the FYP. ("For You Page")

Also, short-form content limits viewers in terms of context. There are many videos in which I have to waste what little time I have repeating the same point as I made in the previous video just so viewers understand the new information I'm trying to show them.

Lastly, not all followers see all my videos. Most TikTok accounts follow 300+ channels. According to Statista, almost 50% of TikTok accounts have more than 5,000 followers, meaning they're likely putting out at least one video per day. (Ceci, Distribution of TikTok influencers in the United States in 2021, by number of followers 2024) Assuming the average length of those videos is a minute, that means every account would have to watch 2.5 hours of new videos per day to stay caught up with the creators they follow. And that doesn't account for the For You Page, watching videos that friends have sent them, or re-watching favorite videos.

And that's just for users who follow 300 channels. Many users follow thousands of accounts. It's impossible to ensure that all your followers watch all your content…

… and that brings me to this book.

I've always been told that my research goes to waste on social media, that I need to reach out to a larger audience or create something to make real change.

Ta-daaaa!

Music intensifies

Writing nonfiction was never on my to-do list, but this is not an ordinary nonfiction book. This book is primarily intended for those who want to learn more about politics in a form that's easy to digest yet more substantial than three-minute lessons on TikTok.

As a result, it's written like my TikTok videos.

Unlike scholarly articles, I'm not focusing on professionalism. I'm not going out of my way to impress those in academia, and although I'm friends on social media with many politicians, I'm not going out of my way to impress them either.

I'm writing this to you.

For you.

Consider this your own personal FYP. Scroll when you want and re-read when you want. Nobody is going to ask you to take a test. (They better not, anyway!) Just learn what you'd like to learn and skip what you don't.

This solely exists so that you can have a broader picture of the data I typically present in my videos, and you can be more confident when you vote in this coming election.

This will be in the same style as always. I'll be responding to claims from commenters, some genuine, some not so much. Like my TikTok channel, this book explores common talking points the average person makes and shows how they hold up in real life with actual data.

Oh, by the way, if you're listening to the Audiobook, just go to my website. I have a complete list of sources and graphs.

All right... now that that's out of the way, let's get to it.

What's the first claim?

Oh yeah, it's...

Party Loyalty

"Vote blue, no matter who!"

Let's start by saying what shouldn't have to be said: Party loyalty is not a political belief.

So many voters in the United States today identify as Democrats or Republicans, assuming those labels show something about their values or morals. However, while expressing your affiliation with a political party might briefly and vaguely sum up your beliefs in the short term, it doesn't address the issue of the long-term change in our political climate.

Affiliation with a political party does not express ideals, reflect morals, or replace individual ideas.

Unlike saying that you are a leftist, a liberal, or a conservative, which describe political beliefs that change slowly throughout hundreds of years according to culture, technology, language, and scientific studies about human behaviors, "Democrat and Republican" political parties, each with their own committees and each with their own platforms, which change every election cycle. (Party Platform 2020)

As a result, by asserting that you align closely with the Democratic or Republican Party, you are saying that you align with the Democratic or Republican National Committee and, therefore, their respective National Convention. By saying this, you're inherently saying you're willing to change beliefs every four years based on the leadership of those organizations, their targeted voter demographics, and the money they receive via political contributions.

Let's put how vast this change is in perspective.

Let's go back, say, nearly 200 years.

Abraham Lincoln, a Republican, was the first president to institute a national income tax.

Why? Because he was very progressive for the time. His policies look quite different from those of Republicans today. If you don't believe me, let's look at a few of his policies and see if they align with those of the modern-day Republican Party.

Revenue Act of 1861:

During the Civil War, the Lincoln administration realized there wasn't enough income to fund the war efforts and needed answers. One of the main problems Lincoln faced was feeding and caring for the soldiers who fought against the Confederates. Providing shelter, food, medical care, etc., was a requirement Lincoln was very vocal about, and he was famous for his view that it was the role of the government to do this.

He went on to say, "One of the greatest perplexities of the government is to avoid receiving troops faster than it can provide for them. In a word, the people will save their government, if the government itself, will do its part." (Nisbet and Nisbet 2011)

The Revenue Act of 1861 was the Lincoln administration's solution to raise additional funds for the Union soldiers. The Act imposed a flat tax of 3% on annual incomes above $800 (equivalent to $356,346 in 2024).

This is quite relevant to the problems we have today. A 2018 study found that 11-30% of our veterans struggle with PTSD. (Kintzle 2018) What's more, according to the Food Research & Action Center, 11.1 percent of veterans between the ages of 18 and 24 live in households that struggle with food insecurity. (Ashbrook 2022)

This isn't a partisan issue; in fact, President Biden signed the Veterans Compensation Cost-of-Living Adjustment Act of 2023 into law, which was delivered by a Congress that unanimously passed it in the Senate. (The White House 2023) Both parties agree that additional funding for veterans is not only needed to take care of the valued members of our military but also required for national security. However, the Republican Party and the Democratic Party have very different plans for instituting solutions to these problems and, importantly, *paying for the solutions.*

With the signing of the Revenue Act of 1862, Lincoln introduced a progressive tax: 3% on incomes between $6000 and $10,000 and 5% on incomes above $10,000. He also established the office of the Commissioner of Internal Revenue. This position later became the head of the IRS and still exists today. He is the president responsible for the framework that created the IRS. (A Century of Lawmaking for a New Nation: U.S. Congressional Documents and Debates, 1774 - 1875 1962) He is also the first U.S. President to impose a tax that only applied to the wealthy. On the other hand, members of the Republican Party today are introducing legislation to reduce funding for the IRS and, in some cases, eliminate it altogether and reduce taxes on high-income individuals and corporations. (United States Congress 2023)

The Republican strategy for paying for the new increases in military costs is to reduce other federal expenditures, while the Democratic strategy is to increase taxation for the wealthy. (Desjardins and Hastings 2022)

While the efficacy of these two strategies is widely debated, it stands to reason that only one matches the executive and legislative style of the Lincoln administration, and it isn't the Republican Party.

The Republican Party that we've had since the 1980s is opposed to taxation. This has been true since George H.W. Bush and was true during the Trump administration. (Trump 2017)

In the words of George H.W. Bush, "Read my lips, no new taxes." (Rothman 2018)

However, that wasn't the only liberal view Lincoln had.

When I speak to Libertarians who claim that Fiat Currency is the core reason for our poor financial situation, yet also claim to vote for the "Party of Lincoln." I feel the need to remind them that Lincoln was the president who signed the Legal Tender Act of 1862, which authorized the use and issuance of paper money. (Glass 2019)

This allowed the United States to print portable, quick, and, most importantly, cheap money. During the Lincoln administration, the US Government used this new paper money to pay off government debts, collect taxes, and fund the war. This was the first step toward fiat money, and it wasn't just the party of Lincoln—it was Lincoln himself.

Let's move on to a policy that would put Lincoln too far left for Liberals today—the Homestead Law.

But before we discuss the Homestead Law and its relationship to our current political climate, it's essential to consider how slavery ended—or, more accurately, *how it didn't*.

Many are quick to forget that we never fully ended slavery. The 13th Amendment says plainly, "Neither slavery nor involuntary servitude, except as a punishment for crime whereof the party shall have been duly convicted, shall exist within the United States, or any place subject to their jurisdiction." (United States National Archives 1865)

The United States does not have a prison system. Instead, the United States has a reformed slavery system. A lot of people draw similarities from our prison system to slavery, but comparison is not where it ends. These two are the same system.

To visualize this, when you compare the population-adjusted prison population of each state today with the slave populations of those same states in 1860, you find that the same states that had high percentages of enslaved people back in 1860 largely have higher prisoner populations today as well. (1860 Census: Population of the United States 1864), (Pariona 2018), (Detailed Data Tool 2024)

Figure 1: Slave Percentages in 1860 as a comparison to Prison Population per 100k in 2024.

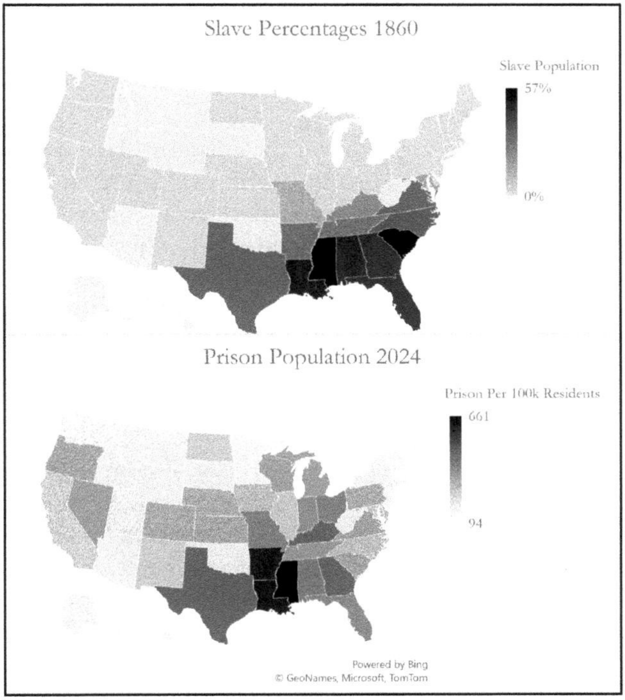

Not only are the geographical similarities striking, but the conversations surrounding the economic dependence on the Prison System are remarkably similar to the reliance on slavery in the 1800's. (Morgan 2020) Just as Confederates argued that ending slavery would hurt the economy and be bad for business, the same conversation exists surrounding prison labor today.

Another striking parallel is the topic of crime rates and revolution. A common argument against prison reform is the idea that criminals will be more likely to revolt or otherwise get away with more crimes. Many believe that crime will skyrocket. Likewise, many believed that if slavery were abolished, enslaved African Americans would revert to "barbarism." (St. George's Institute n.d.)

"If prison labor is illegal, our economy will collapse!"

"We need to keep criminals accountable!"

All these arguments are based on the same ideas and stem from the same source—the fight against the abolition of slavery.

Let's look even deeper.

After the Emancipation Proclamation, slave owners in southern states began losing their workforce and had to come up with creative ways to replace enslaved people without the expenditure of paid labor. Their first strategy was simply not to tell their slaves they were free. In many states, free slaves were still in servitude for up to two years after the Emancipation Proclamation was passed. The holiday Juneteenth marks the day that enslaved people in Texas were finally freed. (Garrett-Scott, Richardson and Dillard-Allen 2013)

This is another parallel to the prison system today. In the United States, prosecutors are required to turn over evidence that could prove the defendant is innocent. However, it's extremely common for this rule to be broken. In 2020, 44% of all exonerations were due to prosecutors withholding evidence of innocence. (Neuman 2022)

However, in 1865, after enslavers were forced to inform

their slaves about the Emancipation Proclamation, their next step was to exploit the loophole in the Constitution and immediately start finding ways to "convert" formerly enslaved people to prisoners.

This was done in many ways. For example, many Southern states enacted Vagrancy laws, which made it difficult for formerly enslaved people to stay out of prison by criminalizing lack of employment and lack of permanent residence. (Tarter 2020) Since they were unlikely to have jobs and permanent residence immediately after being freed from slavery, these laws ensured that formerly enslaved people never left the system.

Laws like this still exist today. (Oxner 2021)

For example, in 2021, Texas passed statewide legislation criminalizing homeless encampments shortly after the city of Austin lifted the ban. However, Texas isn't the only state still implementing legislation against vagrancy. 48 out of our 50 states criminalize homelessness, 24 states have legislation surrounding loitering, and 4 states have legislation preventing sleeping overnight in vehicles. (National Homelessness Law Center 2021)

But back to the 1800's… the next step for the states of Alabama, Texas, Louisiana, Arkansas, Georgia, and Mississippi, which had difficulties finding enough African Americans to penalize, was to start leasing out convicts from other states through the Convict Leasing System. (Terrell 2021) While convict leasing was outlawed by Franklin D. Roosevelt in 1941, the Prison System is still used by over 4,100 companies nationwide. (Classification 50: Involuntary Servitude and Slavery 2016), (Tufts University Prison Divestment n.d.)

All right, now let's get into the Homestead Act of 1862 and how that relates to our current system. Passed on May 20th by Abraham Lincoln, the law provided any citizen or intended citizen who had never fought against the federal government could claim 160 acres of surveyed government land. (Homestead Act 1862) This allowed formerly enslaved people, marginalized communities, and the members of the low class to own land, in many cases for the first time, so long as they lived on and cultivated the land.

I hear you asking, "What does this have to do with our prison system?"

Let's zoom out and consider what the Homestead Act would look like today with our current system. The federal government would be distributing federally owned land to members of those who otherwise couldn't afford it. This includes homeless veterans, for whom our government can't seem to provide and who make up approximately 107,400 people within our prison system. (Maruschak, Bronson and Alper 2021) Government land would also be distributed to marginalized communities and, controversially, ex-convicts who had recently left our prison system.

If legislation like this were introduced today, the "Party of Lincoln" would likely consider it to be Socialist, unconstitutional, and radical—but it was Lincoln's signature that passed it into law.

You may be thinking, "This was Lincoln and the Lincoln administration; it was not representative of Republican values of the time."

But, my dear reader, let me set you straight. Not only was it represented in the Republican Platform of 1860, but that platform also included Plank 14, which stated, "The Republican party is opposed to any change in our naturalization laws or any state legislation by which the rights of citizens hitherto accorded to immigrants from foreign lands shall be abridged or impaired; and in favor of giving a full and efficient protection to the rights of all classes of citizens, whether native or naturalized, both at home and abroad." (National Republican Convention 1860)

Not only was the Republican Party pro-government assistance for people experiencing poverty, formerly enslaved people, and members of marginalized communities, but the party was also pro-immigration and protections for migrants, documented or not.

Also, Plank 12 quite clearly says, "We commend that policy of national exchanges, which secures to the workingmen liberal wages, to agriculture remunerative prices, to mechanics and manufacturers an adequate reward for their skill, labor, and enterprise, and to the nation commercial prosperity and independence."

Simply put, pay your freaking workers.

The Republican Party, back during the days of Lincoln, was the party that promoted wage increases and worker benefits.

In addition, the Homestead Act wasn't limited to the Civil War, the following years, the following decades, or even the century. In fact, the Homestead Act of 1861 remained in effect until the passing of the Federal Land Policy and Management Act of 1976, which was signed into law by Republican Gerald Ford. (U.S. Department of the Interior Bureau of Land Management 2016)

Quick fun fact: At the time of writing, the most recent estimated median age of those living in the United States is 39 years old, meaning half of the population was born during or before the 8th anniversary of the Homestead Act's repealing. (Peck 2023)

Ultimately, the Homestead Act of 1862 allowed government assistance to impoverished families, formerly enslaved people, and marginalized communities. It was signed into law by a progressive, liberal Republican and removed by a conservative Republican more than a hundred years later.

The Republican Party today is not the party of Lincoln.

And these aren't the only examples of Abraham Lincoln's progressive ideals. Suppose you align yourself with the "Party of Lincoln" but also believe in small government, specifically regarding the role of the Federal Reserve. In that case, you don't have the same views about the Federal Reserve as Lincoln did. While Lincoln didn't directly create the Federal Reserve, he signed the National

Banking Acts of 1863 and 1864, which created the first national banking system and created federal regulations on banking, which paved the way for the creation of the Federal Reserve. (Lincoln and the Founding of the National Banking System n.d.)

The same holds true with public transit. Suppose you believe in a small government and disagree with a public transportation system funded and managed by the state with your tax dollars. In that case, you disagree with Lincoln's decision to sign the Pacific Railway Act, which subsidized the construction of the transcontinental railroad.

This was the party of Lincoln: Public transit, taxation, import tariffs, big government, and funding for the impoverished. Does that sound like any Republicans you know?

Also, there are many, many examples of this outside of Lincoln as well.

In 1971, the U.S.A. was entirely removed from the gold standard by President Nixon, a member of the Republican Party, which supports moving back to the gold standard today. (Rimkus 2013)

Also, nearly every Republican president has seen a minimum wage increase during their presidency—with notable exceptions of Ronald Reagan and Donald Trump. (History of Federal Minimum Wage Rates Under the Fair Labor Standards Act, 1938 - 2009 n.d.)

The Republicans in this list include:

1. Dwight D. Eisenhower—the minimum wage increased by 33%, from $0.75 to $1.00. He also taxed the wealthy up to 92%. (Marotta 2013)

2. Richard Nixon—the minimum wage increased by 25%, from $1.60 to $2.00.

3. Gerald Ford—the minimum wage increased by 15%, from $2.00 to $2.30

4. George H.W. Bush—the minimum wage increased by 13.4%, from $3.35 to $3.80.

5. George W. Bush—the minimum wage increased by

12% from $5.85 to $6.55.

At the time of writing, there have only been two Republican Presidents who have not increased the federal minimum wage during their time in office; however, Republicans today nearly unanimously vote against raising the minimum wage.

For example, on July 18th, 2019, the House of Representatives passed H. R. 582, or the Raise the Wage Act, with 228 Democratic votes out of 235 Democrats and only 3 Republican votes out of 197 Republicans. (Roll Call 496 | Bill Number: H. R. 582 2019)

That's why when people tell me that they vote with "The Party of Lincoln," my usual response is, "Ah yes. The party of progressive ideals, taxation, and government assistance! You must be a leftist!"

In my anecdotal experience, they're never quicker to drop support for Lincoln than when taxation or government assistance for formerly enslaved people enters the conversation.

If you say you're a lifelong conservative, that means your views can be described within the definition of conservatism.

If you say you're a lifelong Republican, that means the Republican National Committee, a political organization, dictates your views. When they change their beliefs, you will change with them.

The same holds true with Democrats, who in the 1800s were the party of slavery, conservatism, and small government. Even today, the Democratic Party's views are constantly changing. Let's not forget that Joe Biden shifted from being pro-life to pro-choice just in the span of two presidential administrations. (Liptak 2022)

If you find yourself watching political debates, reading vote records, or listening to President Biden's presidential speeches and thinking that none of these candidates align with your political beliefs, that doesn't mean you're not a conservative, liberal, leftist, etc. It means the political party with whom you had previously aligned has left you behind.

If the party you align with breaks your moral code by front-running a politician you disagree with, your response shouldn't be to adjust your moral code so that you can defend them. Your response should be to find a candidate who aligns the most with your beliefs and vote for them in the primaries. If none of them represent your views in the general election, you are not going against your views to vote against the party.

Quite the opposite.

In 1856, Hannibal Hamlin, a Democrat who was Lincoln's vice president, switched from the Democratic Party to the Republican Party. (Current 2024)

Theodore Roosevelt, a liberal progressive Republican, left his party to create the Progressive Party after clashing with the Republican National Committee. (The Editors of Encyclopaedia Britannica 2024)

Even Ronald Reagan started his career as a Democrat. (History.com Editors 2009)

Your views are separate from political organizations. Please don't tie them together.

No matter where you are on the political spectrum, if these organizations don't represent you, you are doing a disservice to your beliefs by representing them.

However, that doesn't mean that both parties are equally evil, let alone the same. Democrats and Republicans are vastly different than one another. We'll talk about that in the next chapter.

Differentiating the Parties

"Democrats and Republicans are pretty much the same!"

I hear this claim all the time, and not just from online comments. I also hear it in my personal life from people in my family, friends, acquaintances, and occasionally in the news. When someone who identifies with a particular political party loses respect for that party, a common response is, "Both parties are evil."

In my anecdotal experience, these claims are generally from those who don't pay much attention to politics; however, some activists view this way because neither Democrats nor Republicans align with their beliefs. This is also occasionally because they're even further left or right than the political candidates on the ticket, and as a result, these candidates look similar from their perspective.

However, this claim can be tested with empirical data, and when you explore the evidence, there are many categories in which there are stark differences between political parties.

First, let's explore the differences between red and blue states. Why states? Why not cities? Don't worry; we'll cover that later in the book.

For now, we'll start by comparing the statistics of states based on political affiliation determined by four metrics—the 2020 Presidential Election Results (Vestal, et al. 2021), U.S. Senate affiliation (Senators n.d.), U.S. House of Representatives affiliation (Directory of Representatives n.d.), and state governor affiliation (Governors n.d.). These affiliations will be equally weighted on a scale of 0% to 100% Democratic and 0% to 100% Republican. Senate and House affiliations will be measured by the percentage of federal seats occupied by Democratic and Republican representatives, and the Presidential affiliation will be measured by popular vote during the 2020 election. For this exercise, third-party and independent representatives are counted as 50% Democratic.

We can use these percentages to identify where states land on the familiar red, blue, and purple spectrum. States will be grouped into three categories: red, blue, and purple. States that are more than 75% Democratic will count as Blue, states that are 25-75% Democratic will count as Purple, and states that are less than 25% Democratic (or 75% Republican) will count as Red. Here are all 50 states, grouped in order of party affiliation, from blue to red:

Figure 2: List of States Grouped by Affiliation

Blue States:

Connecticut—100% Democratic
Delaware—100% Democratic
Hawaii—100% Democratic

Massachusetts—100% Democratic
New Mexico—100% Democratic
Rhode Island—100% Democratic
Maryland—97% Democratic
Illinois—96% Democratic
Washington—95% Democratic
California—94% Democratic
New Jersey—94% Democratic
Oregon—92% Democratic
Colorado—91% Democratic
New York—89% Democratic
Michigan—88% Democratic
Pennsylvania—88% Democratic
Minnesota—88% Democratic

Purple States:
New Hampshire—75% Democratic
Maine—75% Democratic
Arizona—71% Democratic
Nevada—69% Democratic
Wisconsin—69% Democratic
Virginia—63% Democratic
Vermont—63% Democratic
Georgia—59% Democratic
North Carolina—63% Republican
Kansas—69% Republican
Kentucky—71% Republican
Louisiana—71% Republican
Alaska—75% Republican

Red States:
Ohio—79% Republican
Montana—88% Republican
West Virginia—88% Republican
Texas—91% Republican
Florida—93% Republican
Mississippi—94% Republican

Missouri—94% Republican
Indiana—94% Republican
Alabama—96% Republican
South Carolina—96% Republican
Tennessee—97% Republican
Arkansas—100% Republican
Idaho—100% Republican
Iowa—100% Republican
Nebraska—100% Republican
North Dakota—100% Republican
Oklahoma—100% Republican
South Dakota—100% Republican
Utah—100% Republican
Wyoming—100% Republican

Some of these may be very surprising, but these groupings aren't my opinion; they are mathematical results. For example, Vermont seems like an odd choice for the purple category. Still, Vermont has a Republican governor (About the Governor n.d.) (Phil Scott) and an Independent senator (Bernie Sanders n.d.) (Bernie Sanders) who both brought the political percentage down. Also, more than 30% of Vermont's voters went for Trump in 2020. (Vermont Election Results 2020)

Let's start with crime, specifically rates of generalized violent crime. I've compiled this data from the FBI's Crime Data Explorer, and all these numbers are from the year 2022. (Crime Data Explorer n.d.)

Figure 3: Violent Crime, Homicide, and School Shooting Averages by Affiliation Groups

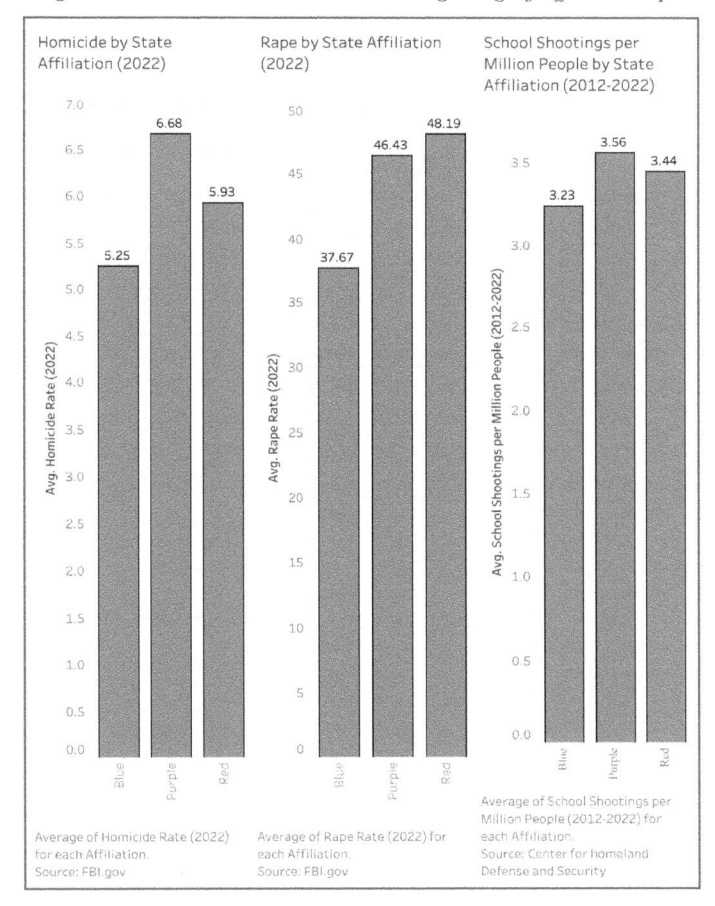

Homicide by State Affiliation (2022)	Rape by State Affiliation (2022)	School Shootings per Million People by State Affiliation (2012-2022)
Blue: 5.25 Purple: 6.68 Red: 5.93	Blue: 37.67 Purple: 46.43 Red: 48.19	Blue: 3.23 Purple: 3.56 Red: 3.44
Average of Homicide Rate (2022) for each Affiliation. Source: FBI.gov	Average of Rape Rate (2022) for each Affiliation. Source: FBI.gov	Average of School Shootings per Million People (2012-2022) for each Affiliation. Source: Center for Homeland Defense and Security

When we examine homicide rates, the average in red states is 13% higher on average than the 5.25 per 100,000 average rate in blue states. When it comes to the homicide rate, purple states are more dangerous on average than blue and red states.

The same phenomenon occurs in school shootings. The data is taken from a compendium of shooting incidents at K-12 schools from January 1970 to June 2022 by the Center for Homeland Defense and Security. For this exercise, I used data from the decade of 2012 and purple states have the highest risk.

Rape rates are lower in the blue states as well. On average, the rate of rape in blue states is 37.67, which is 28% lower than the rate of rape in red states.

So now, looking at all this data, we can see the impacts of legislation in red states versus blue states, and it shows that Republican legislation leads to higher crime rates and higher death rates to a striking degree. As a result, we can safely say that according to the data, at least when referring to risk factors such as crime rates and violence, there is a stark difference between the two parties.

But crime isn't the only metric we can use to measure this. In the next segment, we'll discuss wages, expenses, and the claim that red states are cheaper than blue states.

Affordability of Blue vs. Red States

> "Red states are cheaper to live in!"

With that in mind, we can examine finances and poverty rates between the three categories, specifically regarding income, living expenses, and the amount of money the average family has left over. To do this, I've compiled data from several sources. Let's start with income.

The Bureau of Labor Statistics has monthly summaries of the average weekly wages by state, with percentage differences from month to month and year to year. (Percent change in average weekly wages by state, total covered employment n.d.) After sorting each state into its respective categories, we find that monthly salaries in blue states pay an average of $6,032, or 25% more than in red states, as of September 2022.

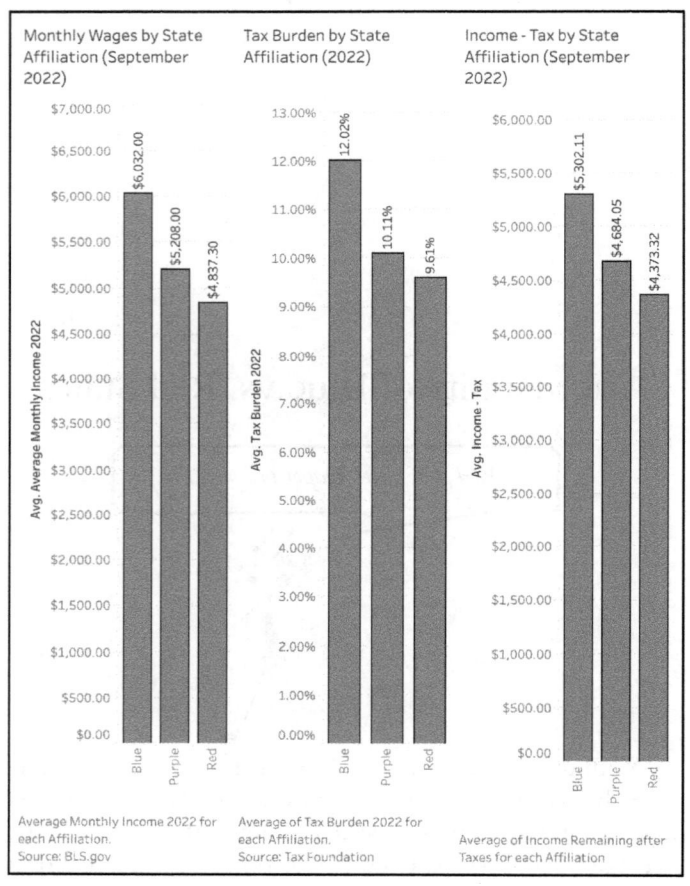

Figure 4: Wage and Tax Burden by Affiliation Group

Monthly Wages by State Affiliation (September 2022)
- Blue: $6,032.00
- Purple: $5,208.00
- Red: $4,837.30

Average Monthly Income 2022 for each Affiliation.
Source: BLS.gov

Tax Burden by State Affiliation (2022)
- Blue: 12.02%
- Purple: 10.11%
- Red: 9.61%

Average of Tax Burden 2022 for each Affiliation.
Source: Tax Foundation

Income - Tax by State Affiliation (September 2022)
- Blue: $5,302.11
- Purple: $4,684.05
- Red: $4,373.32

Average of Income Remaining after Taxes for each Affiliation

This was the most recent time of writing. While this isn't a perfect comparison, since career fields can vary significantly between states, this will give us the most accurate results after we subtract average expenses.

Since these expenses are also averaged across large populations within those states, we can look at what the average person earns and pays for rather than looking at it one career at a time.

The next step is to subtract expenses, starting with Taxes. A common rebuttal in the conversation about income across states and party affiliation is that blue states typically have higher taxes. Hence, those living in blue states make less money after taxes are taken out than those in red states.

To test this claim, I first need to factor in each state's tax burden, which I accomplished by using the effective tax rate of the average person from the Tax Foundation. (State and Local Tax Burdens, Calendar Year 2022 2022)

When sorting these states and averaging their results within their categories, we find a difference in effective tax rates between each group, and the effective tax rate in blue states is, on average, 2.41% more than in red states. In other words, if a family moves from the average red state to the average blue state, they could expect a 25% increase in their effective tax rates. But how does that relate to the discrepancy in income? Do blue states still bring home more money?

As you'd imagine, we next need to find the remaining income after each state's taxes are taken out. When we do, we find that the monthly income after taxes in blue states is $5,302.11 per month, which is $928.78, or approximately 21% higher than the red state average of $4,373.32 per month. Purple states again fall between the blue and red states, with an average of $4,684 monthly.

However, this still doesn't paint the whole picture. Every state also has different legislation that impacts its ability to control living expenses, such as rent, food, and electricity.

First, let's start with rent. To find the average rent cost, I used RentData.org, which compiles the rent rates based on the number of bedrooms, from studio to 4-bedroom homes, from the US Department of Housing & Urban Development. (2023 Rent Data by State n.d.) They then averaged these rates across each surveyed area in the US. These results are for 2-bedroom rental units for the year

2022. The average rent in blue states for this period was $1,203.12, which was around $383.9, or 47% more expensive than in red states. Again, purple states were between the two, averaging $963.85 monthly.

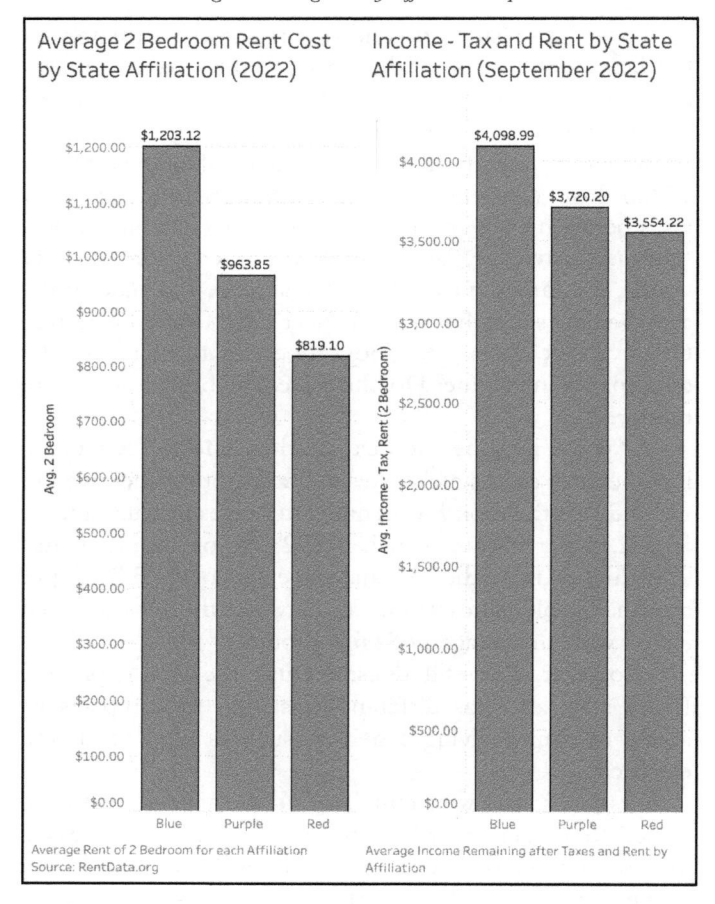

Figure 5: Average Rent by Affiliation Group

Average 2 Bedroom Rent Cost by State Affiliation (2022)	Income - Tax and Rent by State Affiliation (September 2022)
Blue: $1,203.12	Blue: $4,098.99
Purple: $963.85	Purple: $3,720.20
Red: $819.10	Red: $3,554.22

Average Rent of 2 Bedroom for each Affiliation
Source: RentData.org

Average Income Remaining after Taxes and Rent by Affiliation

However, it's essential to remember that although these rent prices might seem striking, they're averages based on all surveyed rental units in each state. A common argument in my comment section is, "Blue states have more urban areas, so they're more expensive than these averages show!"

This claim is partially true. Since rural areas are more likely to be cheaper on average than urban areas, and these results are averaged, the results are likely to have results that are striking to both the urban and rural families in those areas. However, this can vary depending on the state.

Take California, for example. The average 2-bedroom rental unit in California for this period was $1,533, which is much lower than most would expect, even Californians. However, according to the California Forward, the population living in California's rural areas is estimated to be roughly 9% of the population, which means the rural areas in California likely didn't drive down the cost as much as you might think. (Williams 2017)

Compare this to states like Alaska, which is the most expensive red state in the country, in which the average rent price for this period was $1,250 per month. According to the Population Trends and Patterns findings by the Alaska Department of Fish and Game, around 19% of Alaska's residents live in rural areas, more than double the percentage of California's rural population. (Fall 2019)

This leads me to believe that, since rural voters are more likely to vote for Republican politicians (Hartig, et al. 2023) red states are likely to be more expensive than these metrics show for the average person than their blue state counterparts, so if there is any error in this methodology, it's likely making red states seem cheaper, not the other way around.

But, no matter what, it's important to note that those who live in rural areas of a state and those who live in urban areas are still living within the same state, which means the averages between them are still not a reflection of both of these lifestyles, but rather the state itself. I often have comments on social media telling me, "It's the blue cities who drive the prices up!" However, even if this claim were true, these blue cities are still governed by the same legislation and state-wide political representation as rural towns. Big blue cities follow the same state laws as small towns do. You can't discount averages or medians because you disagree with the urban or rural lifestyle.

But moving ahead, even with the increased rent cost in blue states, we need to find out how much that affects the amount of money coming in. So, the next step in this process is to subtract the average rent cost in each state from the average income remaining after taxes. When we do this, we find that the blue states have the most income remaining, equating to $4,098.99 on average. This is about $544.77 on average or roughly 15% more remaining monthly income in blue states vs. red states after taxes and rent are taken out.

Now then, it's time to factor in food costs. For food costs, I found the average cost of groceries from Move.org, which uses U.S. Census data to compile a state-by-state average cost of groceries every year. (Roberts 2023)

In contrast with rent costs, grocery costs are increased in urban and rural areas, with suburban areas being the cheapest (Kaufman, et al. 1997), according to the U.S. Department of Agriculture. This may come as a surprise, but it makes sense when you think about the transportation and distribution of food. Those who live in rural areas typically say that food costs are more expensive in cities and suburbs because much of our fruits and vegetables are cultivated on farms, which can only exist within rural areas. Dairy products, meats, etc., come from rural areas, but contrary to popular belief, that doesn't make the food cheaper.

Typically, even though the food originates from rural areas, it has to travel to industrial areas for storage and distribution before it reaches the customer. Transporting and storing large volumes of perishable goods is expensive and significantly affected by the cost of transportation. (Volpe, Roeger and Leibtag 2013) This means it can be tremendously unpredictable to predict the price of the final good, especially in smaller quantities. In addition, there are very few customers in rural areas. This all contributes to the substantial risk of selling perishables, and as a result, fewer stores exist in remote areas and areas least likely to have large volumes of customers.

On the other hand, transportation costs contribute to the high cost of goods in urban areas. Sitting in high-traffic regions dramatically increases the cost of transportation, not just because of gas mileage spikes but also because of equipment depreciation. City miles are much more demanding on vehicles than highway miles and can significantly increase the cost of transporting goods. The cost increase isn't just from transportation either. Commercial property is also more expensive in urban areas, providing greater business expenses.

That said, unlike the cost of rent, when we factor in the average cost of food between states, it's unlikely that state-by-state legislation affects the cost of goods as much as factors such as population density. This was shown to be true when sorting the average grocery costs of each state within their respective categories.

Figure 6: Average Monthly Groceries Cost by Affiliation Group

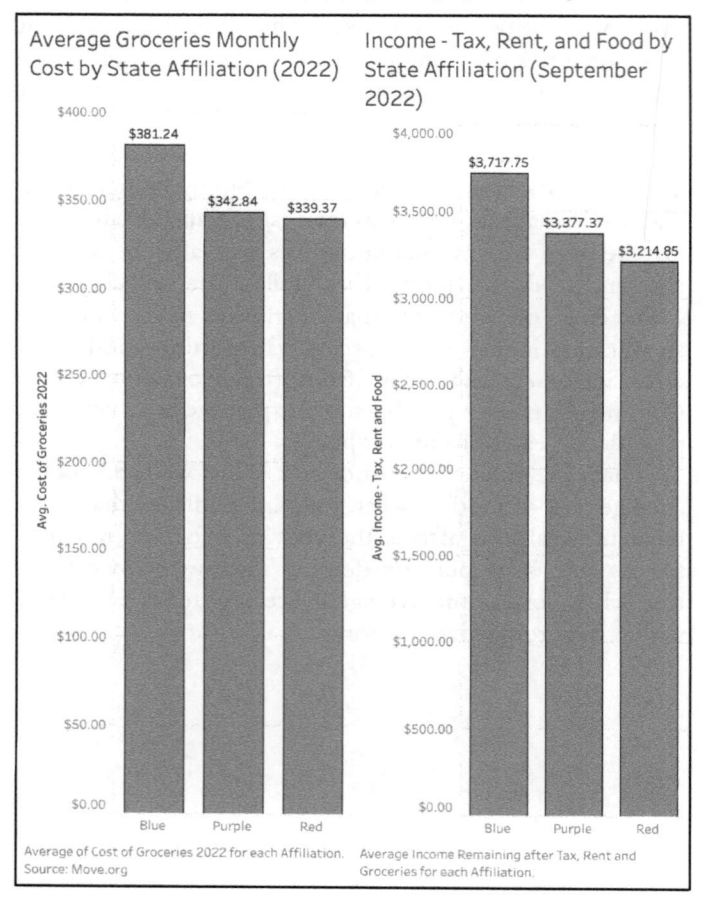

In this scenario, the average grocery cost in the blue states is $381.24 per month. That's significantly higher than the $339.37 in the red states. Families in purple states pay an average of $342.84 monthly on groceries.

Contrary to popular belief, legislation can have tremendous impact on food costs as well. For example, according to the National Institutes of Standards and Technology, 9 states have legislation requiring retailers to post the price per weight of specific perishable goods so that consumers can easily see which items are more worth the money. (A Guide to U.S. Retail Pricing Laws and Regulations 2023) These states are Connecticut, Maryland, Massachusetts, New Hampshire, New Jersey, New York, Oregon, Rhode Island, and Vermont. Using the averaged state-by-state data from Move.org, the average grocery cost per month in states with these regulations is approximately $13.41 cheaper per month than in states without. While this type of legislation doesn't likely bring the cost of each item down, it does allow the customer to make more cost-effective choices when determining which items to buy, saving money on the overall cost of groceries every month.

The last step in comparing these states is to calculate each state's average monthly electricity bills, which I found from the U.S. Energy Information. When gathering this data, I used state-by-state data from September of 2022 because that was the same timeframe as the data for groceries and rent costs in each state were collected. Administration. (Electricity Data Browser n.d.)

When looking at electricity costs, I was surprised that states in all three groups had remarkably similar monthly costs. Red states had the lowest average, around $133.22 per month, and the purple states had the highest average, around $143.67 per month. Contrary to what I'd wager most people would expect, the monthly costs in all three categories are only around $10 apart.

Figure 7: Electricity Monthly Cost by Affiliation Group

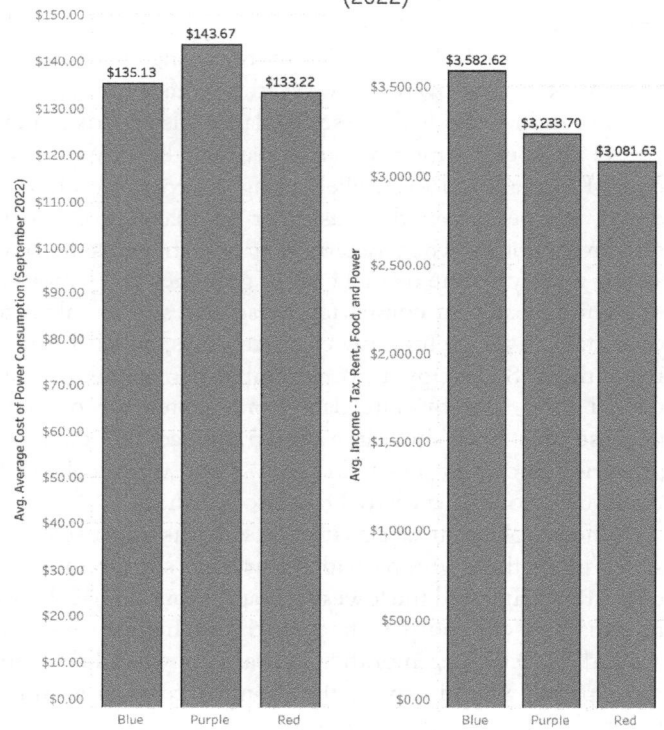

Residential Electricity Cost by State Affiliation (2022)

- Blue: $135.13
- Purple: $143.67
- Red: $133.22

Average Cost of Power Consumption by Affiliation
Source: EIA.gov

Income - Tax, Rent, Food, and Power by State Affiliation (2022)

- Blue: $3,582.62
- Purple: $3,233.70
- Red: $3,081.63

Average Income Remaining after Tax, Rent, Food, and Power for each Affiliation

With this information, we now have a state-by-state comparison of income remaining after taxes, rent, food, and power are all taken out, split into blue, purple, and red affiliations.

And *(drumroll!)* the blue states come out ahead. The average blue state worker can expect around $3,582 remaining monthly after taxes, rent, groceries, and electricity are paid for. This is approximately $348.92, or 10% more than purple states, and $500.99, or 16% more than red states.

You may be wondering why I'm not basing all this data around the percentage of income that these types of expenses cost. There are several reasons for that. To begin, if you factor out rent, groceries, and electricity costs as a percentage of the average monthly paycheck, all three political categories are remarkably similar in percentage. There is less than a 5% difference between the cheapest affiliation group and the most expensive.

Figure 8: Percentage of Income Removed by Taxes, Rent, Food, and Power

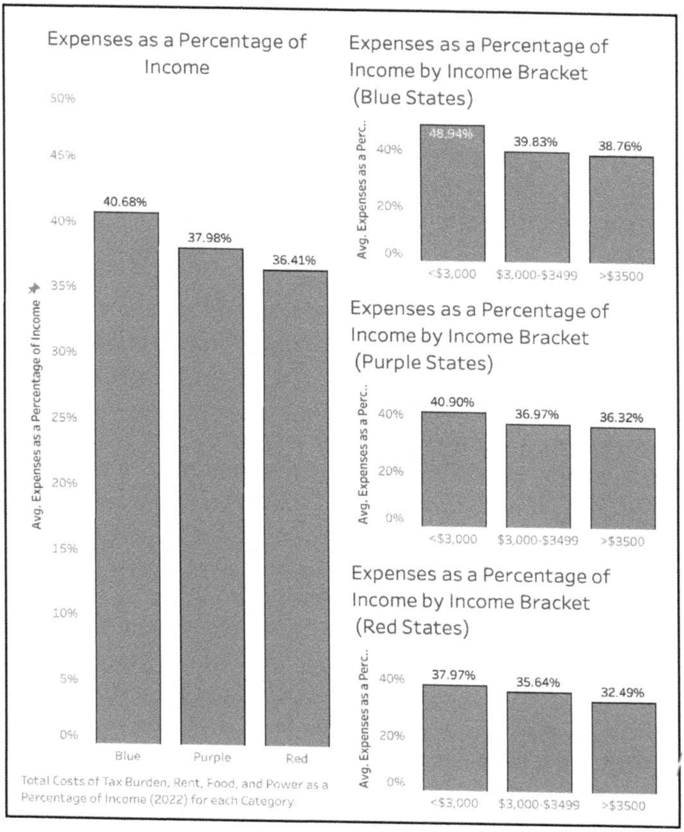

Expenses as a Percentage of Income
- Blue: 40.68%
- Purple: 37.98%
- Red: 36.41%

Total Costs of Tax Burden, Rent, Food, and Power as a Percentage of Income (2022) for each Category

Expenses as a Percentage of Income by Income Bracket (Blue States)
- <$3,000: 48.94%
- $3,000-$3499: 39.83%
- >$3500: 38.76%

Expenses as a Percentage of Income by Income Bracket (Purple States)
- <$3,000: 40.90%
- $3,000-$3499: 36.97%
- >$3500: 36.32%

Expenses as a Percentage of Income by Income Bracket (Red States)
- <$3,000: 37.97%
- $3,000-$3499: 35.64%
- >$3500: 32.49%

Red states are the cheapest. The average red state's expenses equal roughly 36.41% of the average income. Purple states come in second, with expenses taking up 37.98% of the average income. Blue states have the highest expenses as a percentage of the average paycheck, coming in at 40.68%. If you're basing the value of the state on a percentage, that extra 4% of your income goes a long way in terms of safety and quality of life.

Secondly, aside from rent, food, and electricity, the cost of most goods has been equalized due to the impact of online shopping. Most goods, from electronics to toys to furniture to books and even outdoor equipment and vehicles, have seen price equalization across the country. If you buy a laptop, for instance, if the closest electronics store is more expensive than the standard price, most people will buy it online instead. On the flip side, if that laptop is cheaper at that retail store, it'll be purchased online from that store and shipped all over the country. Since the percentage of monthly bills is nearly identical, the percentage of other goods doesn't matter much because prices are also relatively the same.

Thirdly, the average person doesn't determine what they can afford based on the percentage of that expense versus their income; they compare it to the amount remaining after bills are paid. If a family is looking through their budget for December to determine if they can afford a $500 gaming console for a child's Christmas present, they don't think, "Well, my income is about $4,200 per month, so that console is about 12% of my income," they'd take out their monthly expenses and think "I only have $2,000 left after rent, groceries, electricity, etc. So that would bring me down to $1,500." Percentages are a great way to measure the economy from a macro view, but when you look at individual budgets and how much families can actually afford in practice, you need to look at totals as well. A college student making $1000/month but only paying $200 a month to use his friend's spare bedroom still can't afford the same $400/month car payment that someone making $5000/month but paying $1,500 in rent can, even though rent is the same percentage of their income.

In the end, while income percentages still show the stability of one's livelihood because someone paying a higher percentage of their income in rent is less likely to be able to pay their expenses if they lose their income if percentages in all three categories are the same, we can safely use totals.

So, all that said, in response to the claim that Democrats and Republicans are all the same on the economic front, when you look at the impact of legislation and how much the average worker takes home every month, the impacts of Democratic representatives and Republican representatives are vastly different.

We can measure this in several other ways. For example, according to the Bureau of Labor Statistics the most recent preliminary rate of unemployment, which at the time of writing is October of 2023 is approximately 20% higher in blue states than red states. (Berkowitz, et al. 2019)

However, in 2019, the CDC conducted a study linking state-level and county-level healthcare costs and food insecurity. In this study, it's found that red states have much higher rates of food insecurity in both adults and children, despite food costs being similar and unemployment rates being higher in blue states. This can be loosely attributed to the fact that even though blue states have higher wages, they also provide more assistance in the form of food stamps to those who would otherwise have difficulties affording groceries. (Morris 2022)

This leads me to the next topic of comparison—quality and length of employment, specifically how it relates to legislative ideology. Recently, Andrew Van Dam with the *Washington Post* compiled the average rates of employment in each state with data they retrieved from the Bureau of Labor Statistics. In the data, they reviewed the percentage of the workforce within each state who were hired, fired, laid off, or quit within a 12-month period ending in March of 2023. (Dam 2023)

In this examination, the states in which the largest percentage of the workforce gained employment were a part of the purple group, with an average of 4.65%. Red states were the second highest with 4.58% and the blue states on average added 3.96% to the workforce.

However, that doesn't tell the full story. While fewer jobs were added to the workforce in the blue states than in the red states, these states also experienced fewer layoffs and firings than in the red and purple states. Blue states lost less than 1.00% of all jobs over the twelve months, while red states lost 1.08% and purple states lost 1.14%. So, based on available data, workers in blue states are more likely to keep their jobs than workers in red and purple states.

This could be explained by the fact that, according to Gallup, workers who more closely align with the Democratic Party are more likely to be a part of a union than workers who align with the Republican Party. (Newport and Agrawal 2011) Liberal-leaning workers are also more likely to be employed by local and state governments than more conservative workers. This can potentially give liberal workers a greater ability to organize than their conservative peers. As a result, workers in these states are more likely to have bargaining power for higher salaries, better job security, better working hours, and better overall quality of employment.

Figure 9: Job Hires, Layoffs, and Firings by Affiliation Group

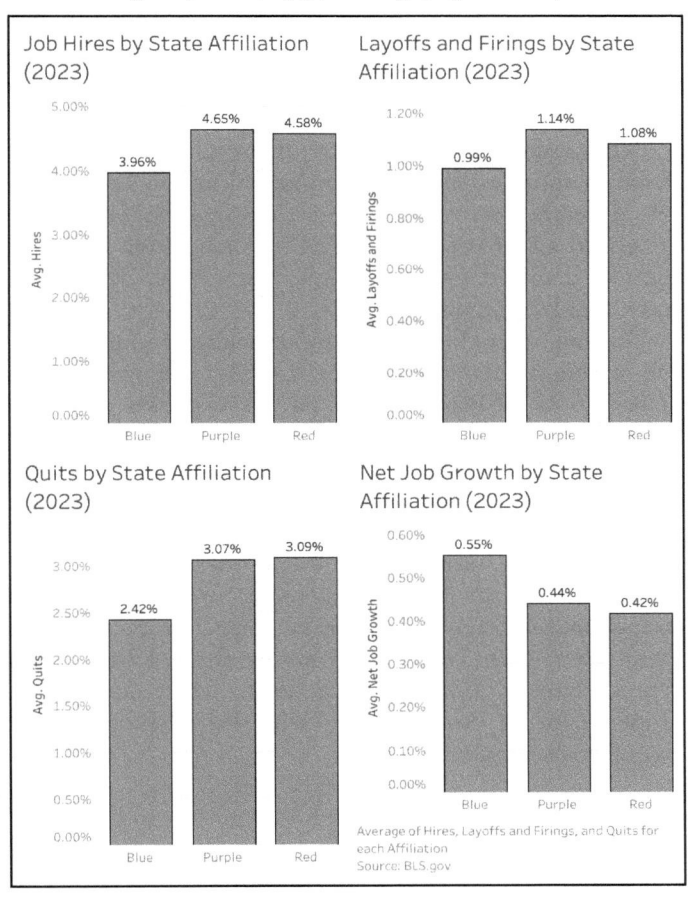

Job Hires by State Affiliation (2023)
- Blue: 3.96%
- Purple: 4.65%
- Red: 4.58%

Layoffs and Firings by State Affiliation (2023)
- Blue: 0.99%
- Purple: 1.14%
- Red: 1.08%

Quits by State Affiliation (2023)
- Blue: 2.42%
- Purple: 3.07%
- Red: 3.09%

Net Job Growth by State Affiliation (2023)
- Blue: 0.55%
- Purple: 0.44%
- Red: 0.42%

Average of Hires, Layoffs and Firings, and Quits for each Affiliation
Source: BLS.gov

On average, approximately 2.42% of workers quit their jobs across the blue state category, in contrast with with 3.07% in purple states and 3.09% in red states. Blue state workers were much less likely to leave their jobs.

With this data, we can measure net job growth by state. By subtracting the percentage of workers who quit their jobs and the percentage of workers who were laid off or fired from the percentage of hiring in every state, we can find out how many jobs were actually created within our three categories on average. However, keep in mind that doing these calculations will likely result in smaller numbers than the original study's margin of error, so take this next segment at face value.

After crunching the numbers, the results are quite close between these categories, narrowing down to less than a .2% difference between the three. However, the blue states generated a higher percentage of jobs per capita in the 12 months than red states or purple states, with .55% more hires than layoffs, quits, or fires.

So, long story short, while the difficulty of getting a new job in blue states and red states is similar, the average blue state is more likely to help you pay for expenses while you search. Not only that, but the job you end up getting is likely to pay higher wages and be more likely to give you secure employment than in purple or red states. Not only that, but workers in blue states are less likely to leave their jobs willingly than in both purple and red states as well.

Therefore, on the employment front, there is a tremendous difference between the impact on red and blue states from their respective Democratic and Republican representatives. With all this data, when looking at employment, it can safely be said that Democrats and Republicans are not the same.

Poverty and Political Affiliation

> *"These issues happen because blue states are less impoverished!"* I hear some of you saying. *"It's a poverty issue, not a political issue!"*

This is such a popular belief and I'm glad you brought it up because when you look at the numbers, you'll find no correlation between these statistics and remaining income.

However, to clarify, this isn't the same thing as saying crime doesn't occur most often in impoverished areas, because studies have shown that within areas of the same or similar legislation, violent crime is much more common in poorer areas.

However, when you factor in states, since states have very different legislation from one another, it tells a very different story.

Figure 10: Homicide and Income Remaining after Expenses

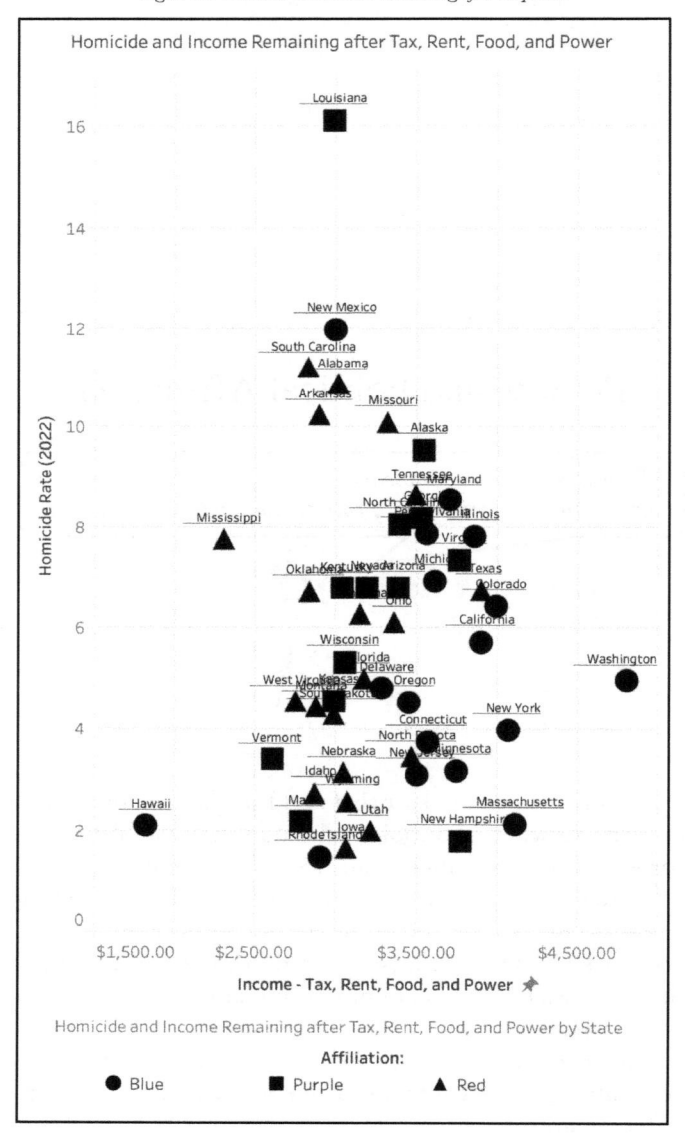

In fact, we can sort this data into income brackets and see how states of different affiliations compare with states of other affiliations within the same income brackets. In the first bracket, all states have under $3,000 remaining after taxes, rent, food, and power. In the second bracket, we have all states that have $3,000 remaining to $3,499 remaining. In the last bracket, we have all the states that have $3,500 remaining and up.

When we do, we find that states with the highest rates of the types of crime mentioned earlier are in the middle bracket, which means these types of crimes aren't limited to the most impoverished states. We can also divide these into the three categories of political affiliation we used in earlier areas of this segment.

For instance, rates of homicide are highest in states with the highest brackets of income in blue states as well as red states. On the flip side, homicide rates are lower in the middle-income bracket in red and blue states.

When looking at rape rates, the lowest income bracket only had the highest rate in the blue states. In both purple and red categories, rates of rape were highest in the highest income brackets.

In the case of all three of these categories, I have found no evidence that these types of crime is higher in more impoverished states. Instead, legislation is much more correlated with related crime rates.

Figure 11: Violent Crime, Homicide, and School Shootings by Groups Based on Income Minus Taxes, Rent, Food and Power

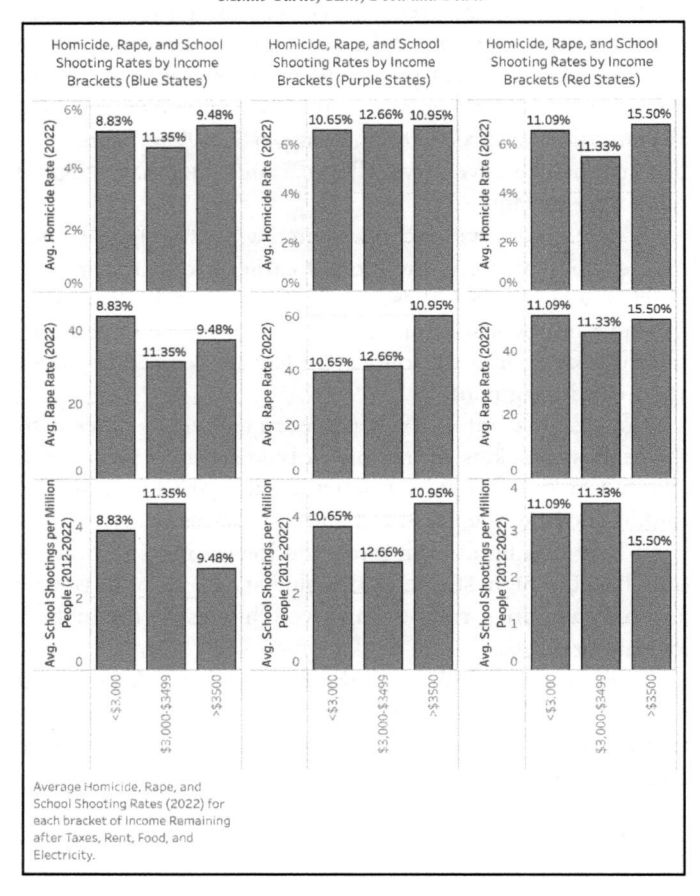

Homicide, Rape, and School Shooting Rates by Income Brackets (Blue States)	Homicide, Rape, and School Shooting Rates by Income Brackets (Purple States)	Homicide, Rape, and School Shooting Rates by Income Brackets (Red States)
Avg. Homicide Rate (2022): <$3,000 = 8.83%, $3,000–$3499 = 11.35%, >$3500 = 9.48%	Avg. Homicide Rate (2022): <$3,000 = 10.65%, $3,000–$3499 = 12.66%, >$3500 = 10.95%	Avg. Homicide Rate (2022): <$3,000 = 11.09%, $3,000–$3499 = 11.33%, >$3500 = 15.50%
Avg. Rape Rate (2022): 8.83%, 11.35%, 9.48%	Avg. Rape Rate (2022): 10.65%, 12.66%, 10.95%	Avg. Rape Rate (2022): 11.09%, 11.33%, 15.50%
Avg. School Shootings per Million People (2012–2022): 8.83%, 11.35%, 9.48%	Avg. School Shootings per Million People (2012–2022): 10.65%, 12.66%, 10.95%	Avg. School Shootings per Million People (2012–2022): 11.09%, 11.33%, 15.50%

Average Homicide, Rape, and School Shooting Rates (2022) for each bracket of Income Remaining after Taxes, Rent, Food, and Electricity.

Blue and Red Cities

"The problem in the red states is the blue cities!"

This is a common argument by conservatives who blame blue cities within red states for the crime rates, risks, and drawbacks of red states. In my anecdotal experience, people seem to use this argument because most news organizations only report on big cities. This isn't a conspiracy, there's a very valid reason for it. Most news organizations have to crunch numbers for cities on a relatively consistent basis, and it's incredibly difficult to compile crime rates for smaller towns. As a result, it's just not worth doing for standard news agencies because there aren't very many people who live in those smaller areas. That extra effort won't be relevant to many people.

In addition, all cities, big and small, fluctuate in crime numbers. However, while big cities aren't greatly affected by fluctuating numbers because the adjusted rates stay relatively the same, a per capita number for a small town can vary greatly.

However, this is a talking point because big cities are almost always blue. When people hear that the bluest cities in their states consistently rank among the most dangerous cities in the country, they think that blue cities have a much higher crime rate than smaller rural areas, and that's just not true.

To examine this, I've gathered FBI data from all cities in 2017, 2018, and 2019, which is currently the most relevant year.

This data includes the rates for murder, rape, and violent crime as a whole. I cross-referenced this data with the 2012, 2016, and 2020 election cycles and put each city in red, blue, and purple brackets.

A spreadsheet with all this compiled data is free on my website.

Let's get to it.

To start, let's look at Texas, the most populous red state in the country and home to some of the largest red cities in the country.

For reference, Plano, the largest red city in Texas, is more populous than Anchorage, four times as populous as Burlington. To put that in perspective, Plano is three times more populous than the capital cities of Vermont, New Hampshire, and Maine combined.

Lubbock, Texas's second-largest city, is 89% as populous as Plano.

Texas has some huge red cities.

Figure 12: Most Populous Red Cities in Texas (2019)

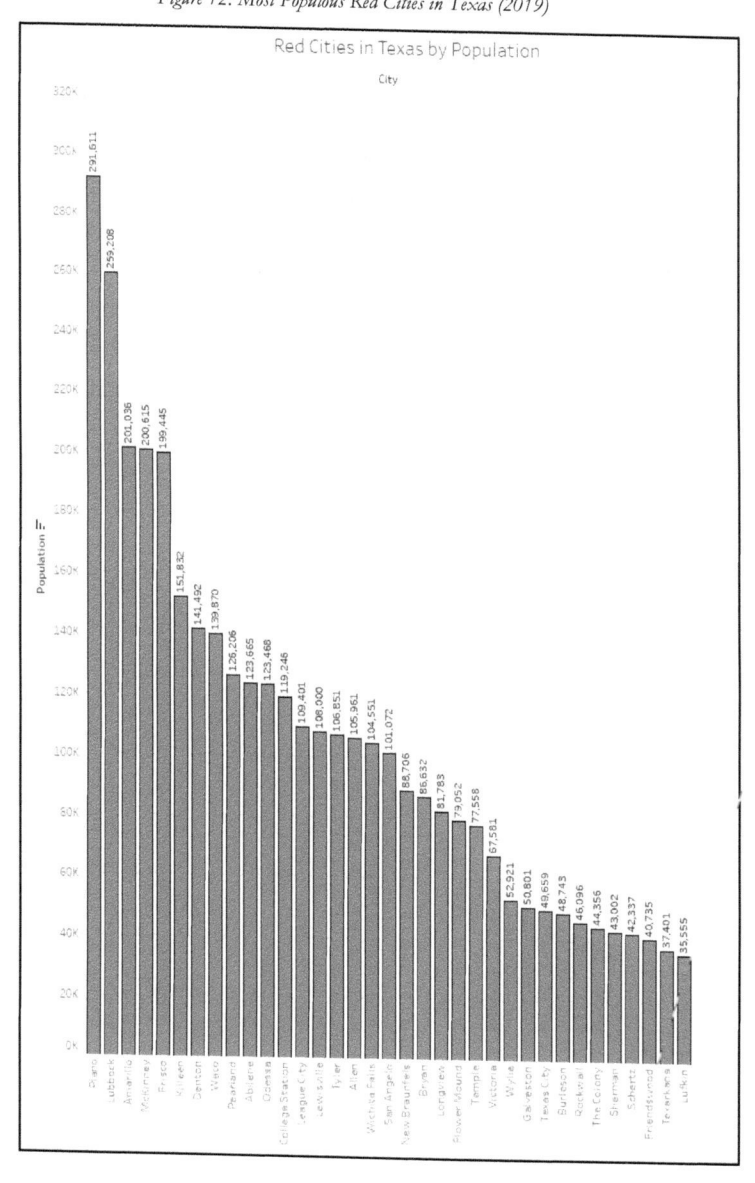

City	Population
Plano	291,611
Lubbock	259,208
Amarillo	201,036
McKinney	200,615
Frisco	199,445
Killeen	151,832
Denton	141,492
Waco	139,870
Pearland	126,206
Abilene	123,665
Odessa	123,468
College Station	119,246
League City	109,401
Lewisville	108,000
Tyler	106,851
Allen	105,961
Wichita Falls	104,551
San Angelo	101,072
New Braunfels	88,706
Bryan	86,632
Longview	81,783
Flower Mound	79,052
Temple	77,558
Victoria	67,581
Wylie	52,921
Galveston	50,801
Texas City	49,659
Burleson	48,743
Rockwall	46,096
The Colony	44,356
Sherman	43,002
Schertz	42,337
Friendswood	40,735
Texarkana	37,401
Lufkin	35,555

Blue and Red Cities | 45

So... are the blue cities the cause of Texas' poor crime rates?

Let's look at the numbers.

In terms of violent crime, blue cities in Texas averaged 314.6 per 100k people over the course of 2017, 2018, and 2019. Red cities were significantly lower, averaging 283.2 per 100k people. However, this is very much dependent on the type of crime. Murders, for example, were 50% more common in the red cities. Rape was 7% higher on average in red cities than in blue cities.

Figure 13: Violent Crime, Murder Rate, and Rape Rate of Cities in Texas by Political Affiliation in 2019

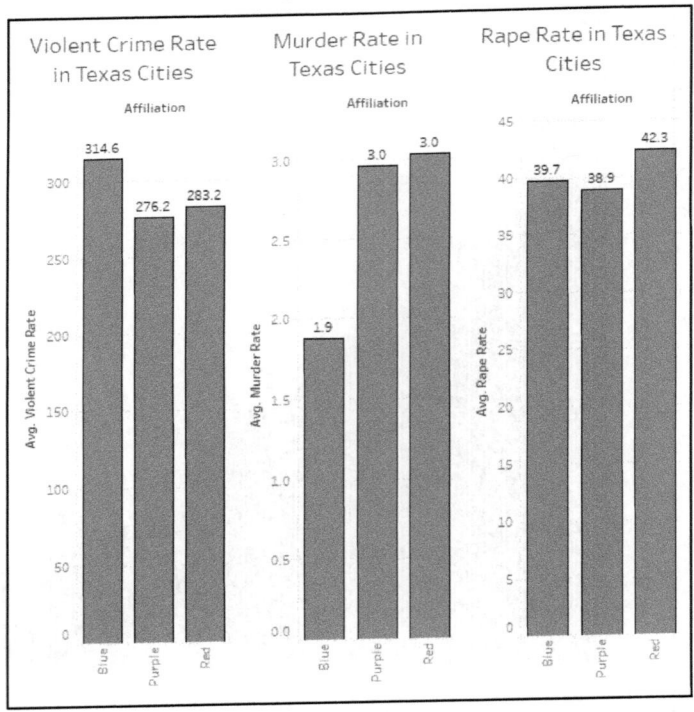

Violent Crime Rate in Texas Cities	Murder Rate in Texas Cities	Rape Rate in Texas Cities
Blue: 314.6, Purple: 276.2, Red: 283.2	Blue: 1.9, Purple: 3.0, Red: 3.0	Blue: 39.7, Purple: 38.9, Red: 42.3

Looking at other types of crime, Aggravated Assault and Burglary rates are relatively even between red and blue cities.

Of all of these stats, the only form of crime that is significantly higher in blue cities than in red cities is property crime, which is more than 50% higher in blue cities.

Figure 14: Aggravated Assault, Burglary, and Property Crime Rate of Cities in Texas by Political Affiliation in 2019

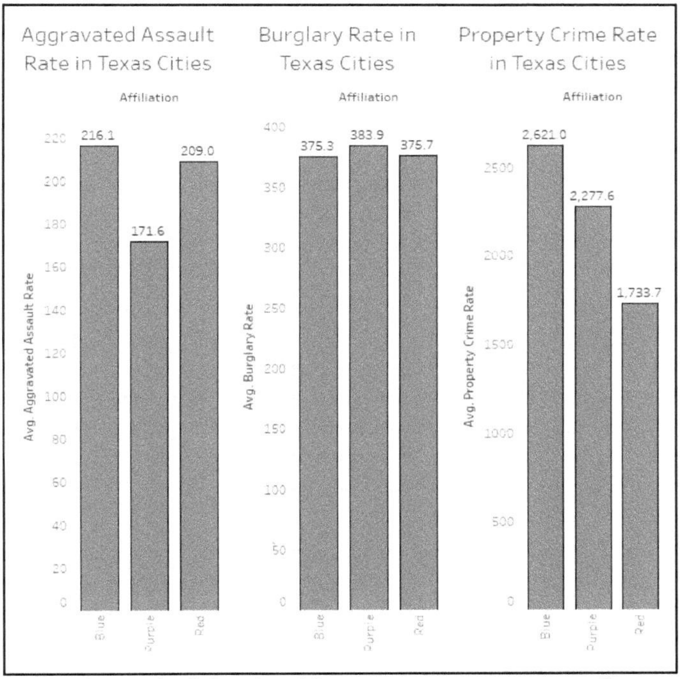

Aggravated Assault Rate in Texas Cities	Burglary Rate in Texas Cities	Property Crime Rate in Texas Cities
Blue: 216.1	Blue: 375.3	Blue: 2,621.0
Purple: 171.6	Purple: 383.9	Purple: 2,277.6
Red: 209.0	Red: 375.7	Red: 1,733.7

At the end of the day, if someone were to move from a blue city to a red city in Texas, they would be trading higher property crime rates for higher murder rates. So, while Texans tend to claim that blue cities are the primary cause of their crime rates, the data simply does not show that.

Again, all this data is free on my website. If you'd like to compile it yourself, you can find it on the FBI website.

But we're not done yet. Let's look at a few more cities.

Since the complaint that blue cities are the cause of crime is common in red states, states with bigger and blue cities must have worse crime rates, right?

Let's look at a blue state. Since Chicago is such a common talking point, let's look at Illinois.

The first thing I want to note is that unlike Texas, the red cities in Illinois are very small. The largest red city in Illinois is Springfield, which has a population of 114,393 people as of 2019.

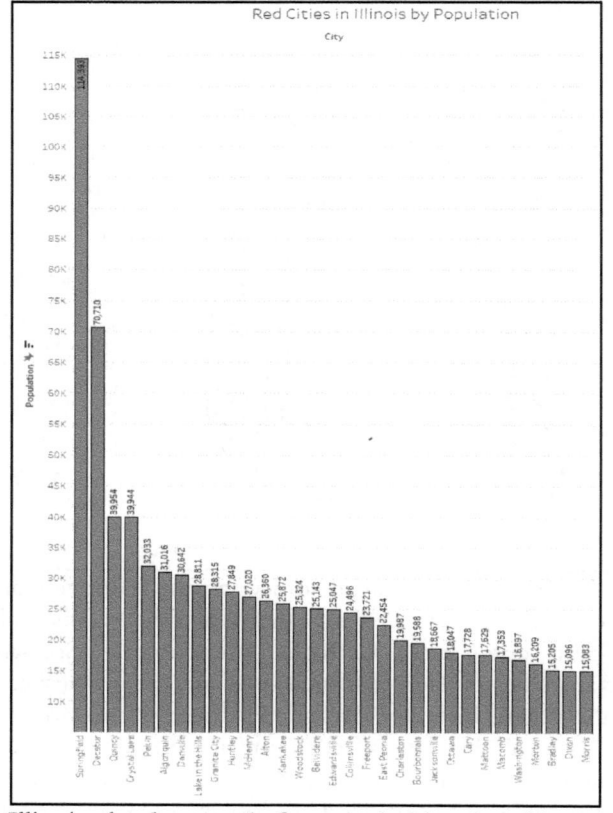

Figure 15: Most Populous Red Cities in Illinois

Illinois also has much fewer red cities than blue cities compared to Texas. Of the cities I measured during this exercise, 697 were blue, and 694 were red in Illinois.

However, Texas had only 380 blue cities and 1594 red cities.

Looking at crime rates, the murder rates, on average, were much higher in blue cities than in red. The murder rate in blue cities was around 4 per 100k people on average, while purple and blue states averaged 1.6 per 100k people.

That being said, violent crime was about even across the state, and the rape rate was significantly lower in blue cities versus red cities.

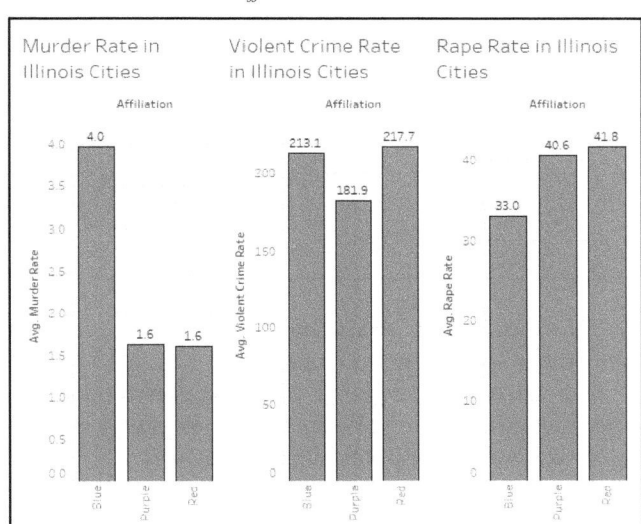

Figure 16: Violent Crime, Murder Rate, and Rape Rate of Cities in Illinois by Political Affiliation in 2019

Murder Rate in Illinois Cities	Violent Crime Rate in Illinois Cities	Rape Rate in Illinois Cities
Blue: 4.0, Purple: 1.6, Red: 1.6	Blue: 213.1, Purple: 181.9, Red: 217.7	Blue: 33.0, Purple: 40.6, Red: 41.8

So, again, while the murder rate is higher, blue cities in Illinois are not necessarily the cause of the crime rates.

In fact, when you look at cities of comparable size, it paints a much different picture.

When only looking at cities with populations higher than 25 thousand people, the crime rates in red cities skyrocket. The murder rate, for example, is 50% higher in red cities than in blue cities. Looking at violent crime and rape, the rates in red cities double that of blue cities.

Figure 17: Violent Crime, Murder Rate, and Rape Rate of Cities in Illinois with Higher than 25 thousand People by Political Affiliation in 2019

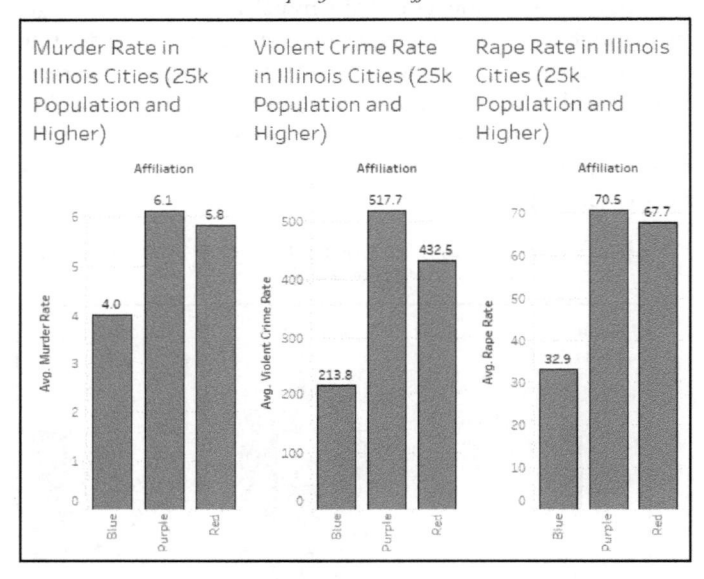

This means that, according to the numbers, blue cities are actually safer than red cities.

But when you get down to it, the conversation about cities being the source of crime isn't necessarily relevant to the discussion about political parties anyway.

The topic of crime and how it relates to political parties is rooted in legislation and the policy choices of either party. When we look at states, we're trying to determine the impacts of legislation passed by liberal and conservative policies, but cities don't typically make up their own policies on large scales. Typically, they're limited in policy by preemption laws, which are laws by the state prohibiting cities and counties from passing legislation that the state doesn't approve of.

For example, only eight states allow cities to create specific types of firearm legislation. (Every Town Research n.d.)

The Economic Policy Institute also has a page that shows the states that have preemption laws for workers' rights as well. (Workers' rights preemption in the U.S. 2024)

However, in contrast to states, people who focus on cities are primarily focused on people instead of legislation. Instead of comparing the consequences of liberal and conservative *policies*, they're concerned with blaming problems on liberal or conservative *people*. It's not about whether democratic policies are ineffective; it's about whether *liberal and left-leaning voters* are causing the problems. But the thing is, not only is that not a productive conversation, but the claim that Democrats are bad people and criminals are more likely to be Democrats is also demonstrably false.

We have asked convicted felons about their political beliefs and ideals.

The Marshall Project, a nonprofit criminal justice journal, surveyed 8,000 convicts in our criminal justice system in 2020 and asked who they would vote for. (Lewis, Shen and Flagg 2020)

The data was split into two categories based on race.

When it comes to party affiliation, it was primarily split down racial lines. 36% of white respondents said that they align with the Republican Party, 30% said that they align with Independents, and only 18% said they align with the Democratic Party.

For Black respondents, the numbers were almost nearly reversed. 45% of Black respondents said that they identify with the Democratic Party, 29% they identify with independents, and 11% said they identify with the Republican Party.

So, not only do the results of that study show that convicted felons aren't inherently more likely to be associated with the Democratic Party, but the results regarding specific candidates and policies show the exact opposite.

According to the survey about preferred political

candidates, the largest political opinion of people of color was "Don't know/would not vote" at 29%. 19% of the respondents who were people of color said that they would vote for Donald Trump, 16% said that they would vote for Bernie Sanders, and only 13% of them said they would vote for Joe Biden.

White respondents were much less divided, with 45% saying they would vote for Donald Trump, 25% saying they don't know or would not vote, 10% saying they would vote for Bernie Sanders, and only 7% saying they would vote for Joe Biden.

In the same survey, they asked about policies around tightening the border. 81% of respondents who identified as Republicans supported tightening border security, while only 9% opposed the idea. On the other side, 44% of respondents who identified as Democratic supported tightening border security, but only 30% opposed it.

So, the bottom line is even though many convicted felons say that they support the Democratic Party, they're more likely to vote for Republican candidates, and they're more likely in favor of Republican policies. And again, policy is the most important part.

However, keep in mind that prisoner affiliation is not helpful in the discussion of systemic or systematic problems. It's not really important to bring up who the "bad people" are anyway.

When you're comparing the Democratic and Republican parties, the most effective means of comparison is the impacts of the policies passed by Democratic and Republican representatives. This can only be achieved reliably and thoroughly on the state and national level since cities are largely unable to make policies about much of what causes problems within those cities.

The data doesn't lie; when you look at the statistics at the state level, the Democratic states perform better in nearly every category.

In the next chapter, we're going to look at

statistics related to raising a family within these states. This includes education quality, rates of maternal and infant mortality, teen pregnancy rates, sexual assault rates, and more.

Raising a Family in Red vs. Blue States

"Red states are better for raising a family!"

Let's look at raising a family in these states. We'll go through the whole process, starting from getting pregnant and having a baby. We'll then move to the quality of that child's life throughout their education and look at graduation rates.

Let's start with the first part of having a child, getting pregnant, and having a baby. To begin this category, we'll look at maternal mortality rates. These statistics are from the CDC and include rates for each state from 2018 to 2021. (Maternal deaths and mortality rates: Each state, the District of Columbia, United States, 2018-2021 n.d.)

After sorting these states into their respective affiliation groups, we find that red states have nearly twice the risk of maternal mortality as their blue state counterparts. The average maternal mortality rate in red states is 30.72 per hundred thousand, while blue states average around 18.49. Purple states are again in the middle, with around 28.18 per hundred thousand.

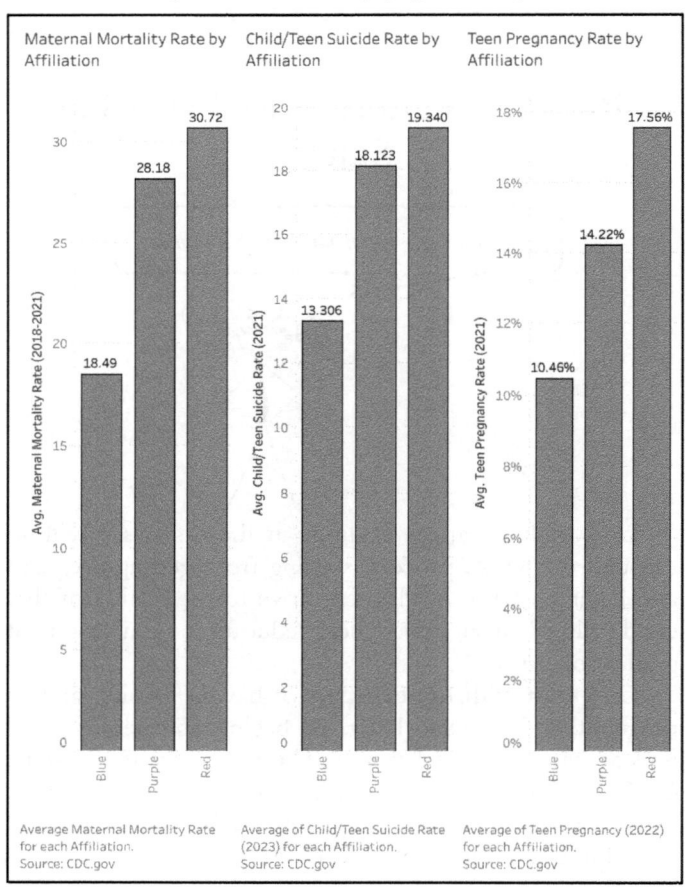

Figure 18: Maternal Mortality by Affiliation Group

So, to begin, if a family plans on having a child, the safest place on average to carry the pregnancy and give birth is in a blue state.

Next, we'll look at quality of life and education.

We've already talked about school shooting numbers by political affiliation, so we know that public school is a much safer environment in blue states than it is in red states, but we also need to address another uncomfortable metric—child and teen suicide rates.

While this is not something we want to think about, it is an important conversation. Over the last 17 years, suicide rates for America's youth have increased by 62%. (Shrikant 2023) There have been many documented reasons for this, including global conflict, rapid inflation, higher costs of living, and many other factors. However, since these factors can't be measured or correlated by a single metric, it's essential to find a way to create a happy home for children, and part of that puzzle is to locate the areas in which the risks of suicide in youth are lowest.

This data was gathered by the CDC and represents the suicide rate for youth and teens from age 10 to 17 from the year of 2022, the most recent data available at the time of writing. (Suicide Rates by State 2023)

After sorting the data, the difference based on political affiliation is, once again, very jarring.

The average suicide rate for 10 to 17-year-olds across red states is 19.34 per 100k, which is nearly 50% more than the suicide rate for their blue-state counterparts. Once again, purple states fall between them at 18.12 per 100k.

While we're on the subject of quality of life for our youth, we need to look at another uncomfortable statistic—teen pregnancy.

This data was also compiled by the CDC and contains the Teen Pregnancy data for the year 2021, which, at the time of writing, is the most recent data available. (Teen Birth Rate by State 2022) Like many other categories, red states are the highest affiliation group regarding average teen pregnancy rates, with 17.56 births per 1000 young women. Purple states are in the middle, with 14.22 per thousand, and blue states have the lowest, with 10.46.

Now, let's talk about your ability to feed your children.

Figure 19: Food Insecure Children by Affiliation Group

We've already gone over income and expenses, but what about food insecurity? According to the U.S. Department of Agriculture's Economic Research Service, Food Insecurity doesn't just include food prices in individual areas. (Definitions of Food Security n.d.) Instead, it's primarily the ability to access that food. There are many areas wherein residents have the financial buying power to afford food but don't have access to it either by means of transportation or food availability within a reasonable distance. As a result, areas with high food insecurity aren't necessarily the same areas with financial roadblocks when buying food.

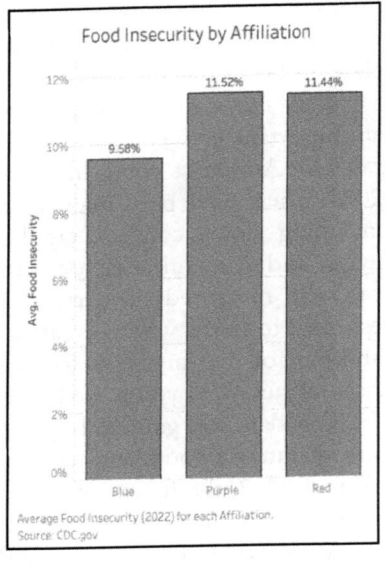

According to the Economic Research Service, purple states have the highest rates of food-insecurity, averaging 11.52%. Red states have the second highest rates, at 11.44%, and blue states have the lowest rates, at 9.58%. (Prevalence of food insecurity, average 2020-22 2023)

Now, let's look at the quality of education. For this segment, we'll be looking at SAT results. These scores were gathered by Prepscholar, who compiled data from CollegeBoard's 2022 SAT state reports. (Cheng n.d.) When we examine the data, we find that in contrast with most metrics we've observed, red states score higher than blue states on ERW and Math scores on average, with red states averaging out at 549.9 for Math and 567.06 for ERW. However, purple states lead with 561.23 for Math and 578.92 for ERW.

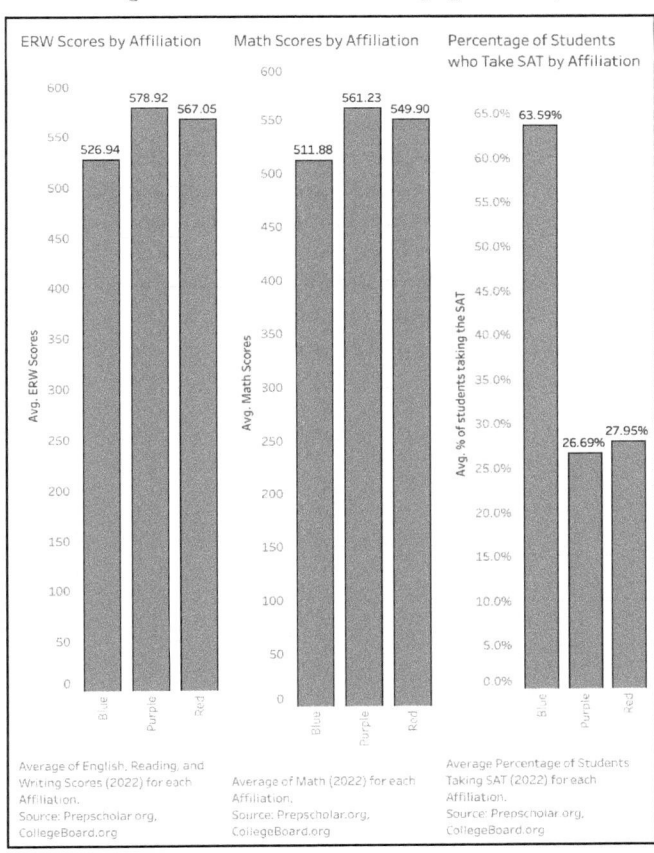

Figure 20: SAT ERW and Math Scores by Affiliation Group

However, this can be partially explained by the fact that, according to PrepScholar, blue states disproportionally require students to take the SAT, even if they're not necessarily ready or would otherwise elect not to. (Heimbach n.d.) This results in a vast difference in the percentage of SAT students in each state. Blue states have the highest average rate of students who take the SAT, with 63.59%. Red states come in a distant second with an average of 27.95% of the children taking the SAT, and purple states have the lowest average with 26.69%.

This implies that in blue states, many of these lower test results are because students who are either not ready or unwilling to take the test are required to, and their performance artificially lowers the average.

At the end of the day, when we measure the many metrics and data points surrounding raising a child in red, blue, and purple states, it's safe to say that, on average, in blue states, it's safer to have a child, it's safer for the child, the child is more likely to be safer as they grow up, they're more likely to have better mental health, and they're more likely to get a well-rounded education.

Funding to Democrats vs. Republicans

"Democrats and Republicans are funded by the same people!"

This is another common argument and one that seems to be widespread, especially on social media. The argument stems from the fact that both parties continue to get more conservative and Democratic politicians are no longer a reflection of the stats of their state or the legislation in that state. I can see the argument here because, as I mentioned in the first chapter, political parties constantly change.

However, the argument that Democratic and Republican politicians are the same still doesn't hold water when you look at the numbers, especially when you look at political funding. Let's dive into political donations from organizations, including those funneled through PACs and SuperPACs, and compare the political affiliations of the candidates who receive those donations. All of this data is tracked and compiled via OpenSecrets, a nonprofit organization that specializes in tracking dark money sent to politicians. I'll specifically use data from the 2020 election since that's the most recent presidential election and the most relevant to this coming election in 2024.

To start, let's look at the most obvious example—Gun Rights Activists.

According to OpenSecrets, the largest sum of Gun Rights donations was from the NRA, which had 81% of the total contributions from Gun Rights groups. The NRA donated over $9 million to political candidates and groups in 2020 alone. The second highest was the National Shooting Sports Foundation, which donated $1 million, or around 10% of the total.

Figure 21: Political Funding from Gun Rights Activist Groups in 2020

Gun Rights Activist Groups

- National Rifle Assn
- Gun Owners of America
- National Shooting Sports Foundation
- Safari Club International
- National Assn for Gun Rights
- Dallas Safari Club
- Ohio Gun Collectors Assn
- Delta Defense LLC
- EAGLE GUN RANGE

SOURCE: Opensecrets.org
(Gun Rights Summary 2021)

Given the massive totals of these donations, how much was spent on Democrats and Republicans? Well, out of the $11.3 million total funding from Gun Rights activist groups,

$1.9 million went to candidates themselves, and out of that total, only $35 thousand went to Democratic Candidates, or about 0.3%.

Figure 22: Political Funding from Gun Rights Activist Groups by Party in 2020

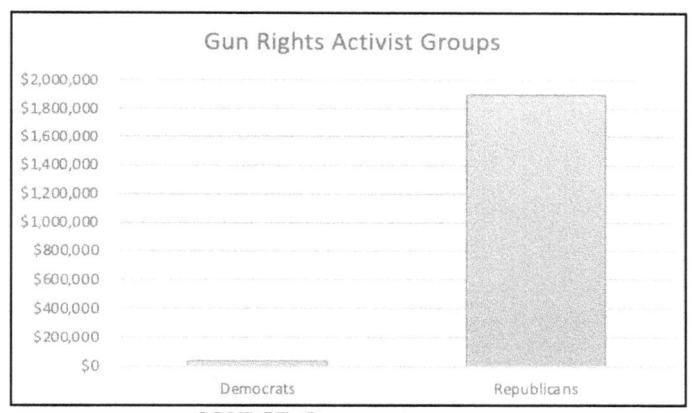

[Bar chart titled "Gun Rights Activist Groups" showing Democrats with a negligible bar near $0 and Republicans with a bar reaching approximately $1,850,000.]

SOURCE: Opensecrets.org
(Gun Rights Summary 2021)

Where did the rest of the money go? It went to other political groups. For those following along at home, the remaining $9.3 million, the vast majority of the political spending money, went to conservative groups. We don't even need a graph for this one because liberal groups got a fat goose egg, 0$, from Gun Rights Activist groups.

This may be common sense, but when it comes to Gun Rights Activists, Democrats and Republican politicians are far from equal.

Let's move on to the next industry, For-Profit Prisons.

According to OpenSecrets, For-Profit Prisons spent a total of $3 million toward political contributions during the lead-up to the 2020 election. 84% of that $3 million was donated by the GEO Group, which donated a total of around $2.6 million. The second highest organization when it comes to political funding was Core Civic, which donated $360 thousand. Their contributions were around 12% of the total.

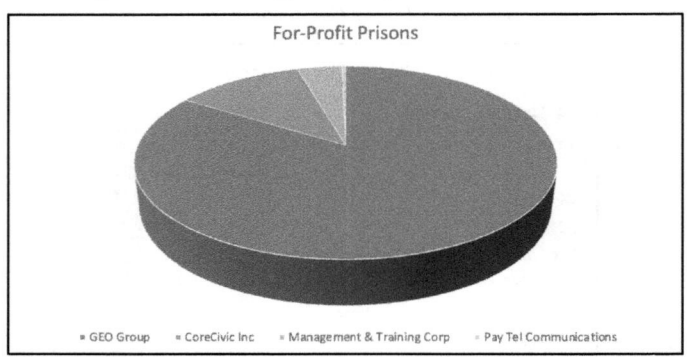

Figure 23: Political Funding from For-Profit Prisons in 2020

[Pie chart: For-Profit Prisons — GEO Group, CoreCivic Inc, Management & Training Corp, Pay Tel Communications]

SOURCE: Opensecrets.org
(For Profit Prisons 2021)

When we break it down by political party, we find that around $2.9 million went to political candidates. Out of that money, $193 thousand went to Democrats and around $1.9 million went to Republicans.

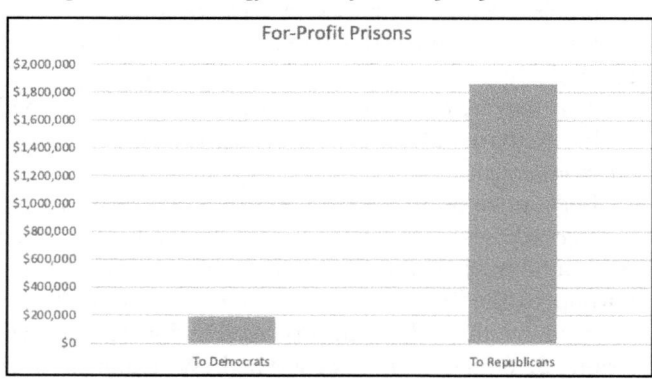

Figure 24: Political Funding from For-Profit Prisons by Party in 2020

[Bar chart: For-Profit Prisons — To Democrats (~$193,000), To Republicans (~$1,850,000)]

SOURCE: Opensecrets.org
(For Profit Prisons 2021)

Let's move on to the Oil and Gas industry, the biggest industry we've covered so far. At the time of writing, Oil and Gas is the 5th largest industry for political contributions in the country. In the 2020 election cycle alone, the top 20 companies in the industry spent nearly $79 million in political contributions.

The top contributor was Energy Transfer LP, the owner of Sunoco. They spent around $15 million or 19% of that total. The second highest was Koch Industries, which spent $13 million, or around 17% of the total.

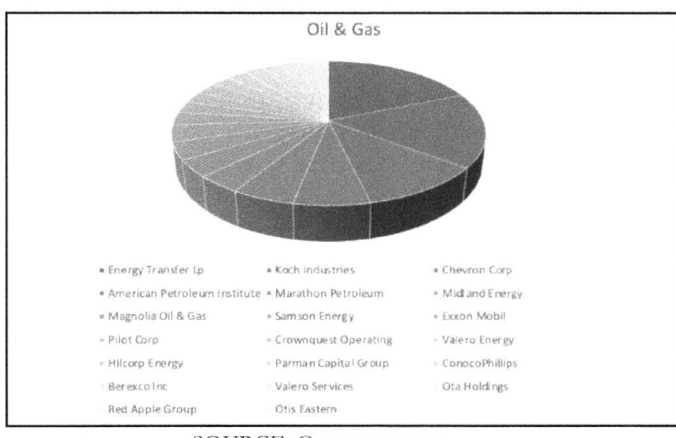

Figure 25: Political Funding from the Oil and Gas Industry in 2020

SOURCE: Opensecrets.org
(Oil & Gas Summary 2021)

Out of the $79 million total, a total of $27 million was spent on candidates. Breaking it down by political party, we find that only $3.4 million went to Democrats and $23.6 million went to Republicans.

Figure 26: Political Funding from the Oil and Gas Industry by Party in 2020

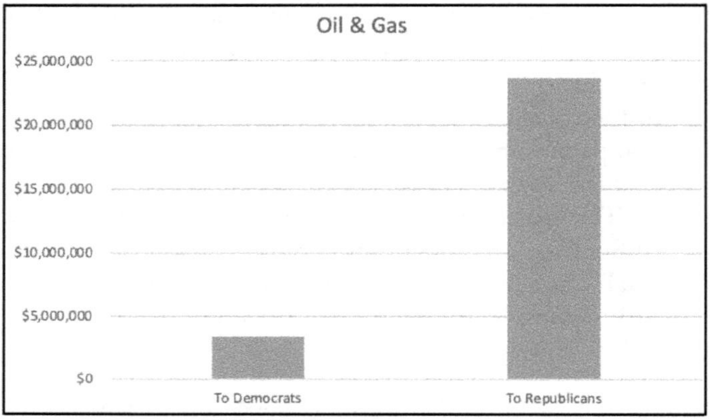

Oil & Gas
$25,000,000
$20,000,000
$15,000,000
$10,000,000
$5,000,000
$0
To Democrats
To Republicans

SOURCE: Opensecrets.org
(Oil & Gas Summary 2021)

When it comes to interest groups, it paints a similar picture. $2.7 million was donated to liberal-leaning groups and $49.2 million was donated to conservative groups.

Figure 27: Political Funding from the Oil and Gas Industry by Political Groups in 2020

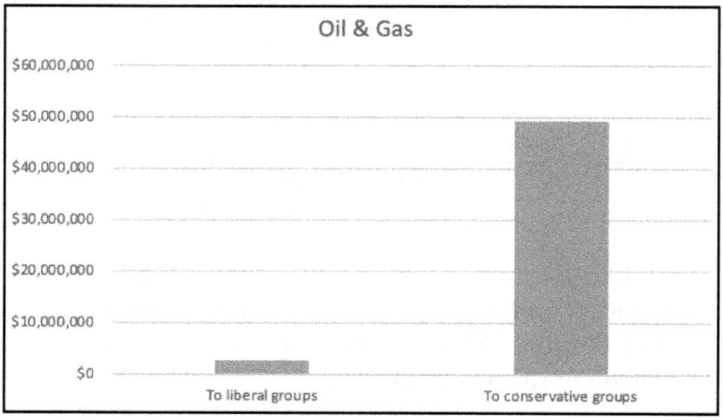

Oil & Gas
$60,000,000
$50,000,000
$40,000,000
$30,000,000
$20,000,000
$10,000,000
$0
To liberal groups
To conservative groups

SOURCE: Opensecrets.org
(Oil & Gas Summary 2021)

However, all of these are industries that are universally known to lean conservative. It shouldn't be a surprise to anyone that Republicans receive more money from Gun Rights Activists, For-Profit Prisons, and the Oil & Gas industry. What about some controversial groups? What about the sources of political contributions that muddle the water for the argument that Democrats and Republicans are inherently opposing parties?

Let's look at... AIPAC funding. For those who don't know, AIPAC stands for the American Israel Public Affairs Committee. They have been the subject of many debates and conversations surrounding the events in Palestine, specifically Gaza. Democrats have primarily been heavily criticized for the response to Israel's attacks because AIPAC has spent more money on political funding for Democrats than they have for Republicans. Democrats across both chambers received a total of $5.6 million from AIPAC, while Republicans only received $4.4 million.

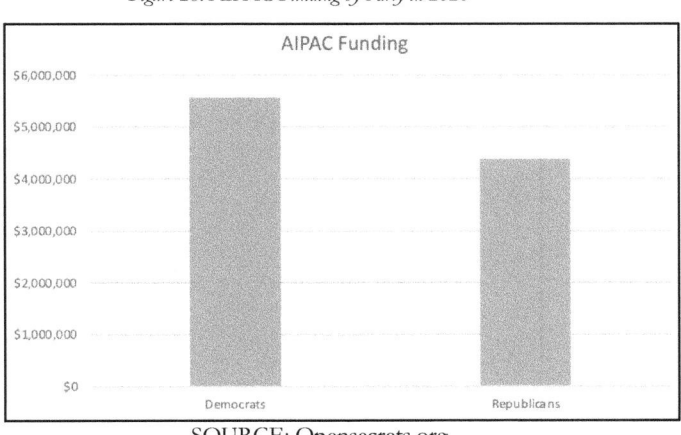

Figure 28: AIPAC Funding by Party in 2020

SOURCE: Opensecrets.org
(American Israel Public Affairs Cmte 2024)

However, while this appears to show that Democrats and Republicans are funded by AIPAC evenly, this doesn't paint the full picture. Unlike the other three categories, the spread of individual politicians matters a great deal when it comes to funding from AIPAC funding. In the 116th Congress, the Republicans controlled the Senate, and the Democrats controlled the House. Combining both chambers, there was a total of 277 Democrats and 250 Republicans in Congress.

Why does that matter? Because there were 10% more Democrats in office. Meaning, that even if AIPAC treated both parties equally, the total going to Democrats would still be higher. However, they did not treat Democrats and Republicans equally. Republicans were much more likely to receive AIPAC money than Democrats were.

Across both chambers, 250 Republicans received money from Israel's committee, however on the Democratic side, only 136 of all Democrats received money from the committee. Long story short, nearly 80% of all Republicans received money from AIPAC while less than half of the Democrats did.

Figure 29: Percentage of Candidates Receiving AIPAC Funding by Party in 2020

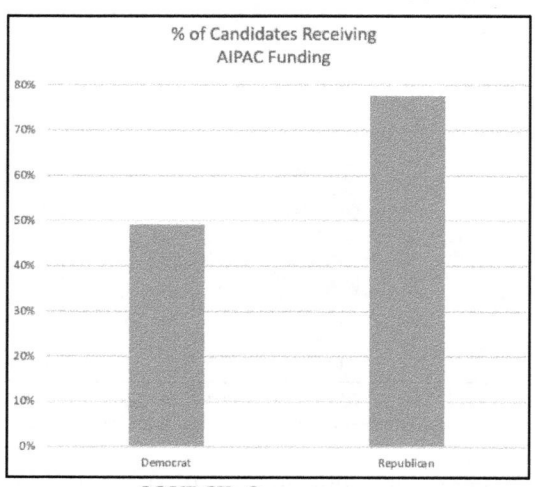

SOURCE: Opensecrets.org
(American Israel Public Affairs Cmte 2024)

What does that mean? That means that the Democrats who are pro-Israel typically receive more funds on average than Republicans who are pro-Israel, but more than half of the Democrats in the 116th Congress did not receive money at all.

So, yes. This is a huge difference. No matter what your stance is on Israel or its actions, it's safe to say that the party that you vote for does affect Israel's say in American politics.

So, you may be asking, what are the groups who primarily donate to Democrats? Well, one of the largest industries is Education, in which the top 20 universities alone donated $95.5 million during the 2020 election cycle. More than a quarter of that was donated by the University of California, who donated $25.2 million and $19.4 million of that was to Democrats.

When we compare the total donations of the top 20 donors across both political parties, we find that nearly $81 million went to Democrats, and only $3.6 million went to Republicans.

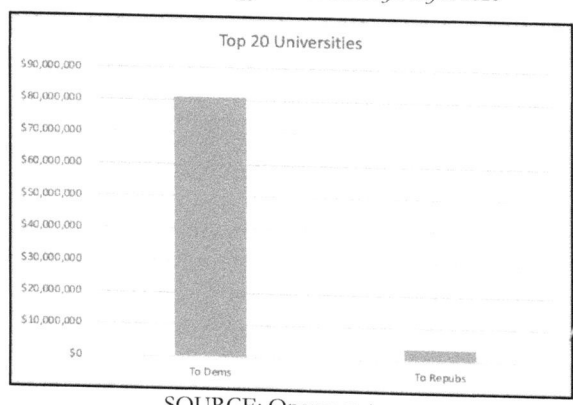

Figure 30: Political Funding from Universities by Party in 2020

SOURCE: Opensecrets.org
(Education Summary 2021)

When comparing donations to political groups, we find similar results. $9.9 million was donated to liberal groups and only $58.9 thousand was donated to conservative groups.

The same holds true for Public Sector Unions. The top 20 unions donated a combined 92.7 million to candidates during the 2020 cycle and the union with the most donations was the National Education Association, which donated $48 million, more than the rest of the top 20 unions combined.

Comparing the two parties, Democrats received $18.6 million in donations while Republicans only received $2 million.

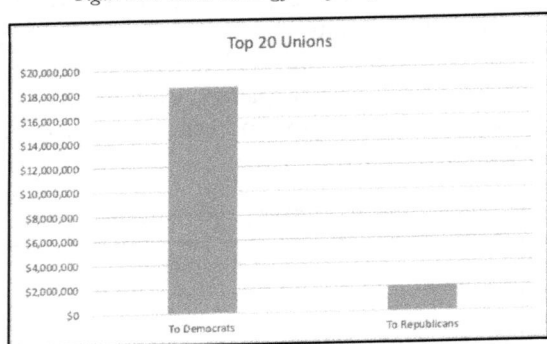

Figure 31: Political Funding from by Party in 2020

[Bar chart titled "Top 20 Unions" showing approximately $18,000,000 To Democrats and approximately $2,000,000 To Republicans]

SOURCE: Opensecrets.org
(Education Summary 2021)

As you might have guessed, donations to political groups are very similar. In the 2020 election cycle, top 20 unions donated $10,000 to conservative groups and over $71.8 million to liberal-leaning groups—well over 700 thousand times the amount.

Now, Democrats aren't all sunshine and rainbows and they do get similar funding as Republicans in some areas. Some industries that donate to Democrats and Republicans aren't nearly as universally beloved as teachers' unions. As an example, let's look at securities and investment companies—you may know a few of these as hedge funds. This industry is the largest when it comes to political donations and some of these numbers might surprise you.

The top twenty securities and investment companies donated a total of nearly $449 million in the 2020 election cycle. The top contributor, Fahr LLC/Tom Steyer donated a total of nearly $70.8 million.

Breaking down the political affiliation for the donations of the top twenty security and investment companies, Democrats get the highest amount of donations. Around $18.2 million was given to Republicans and almost $26 million went to Democratic candidates.

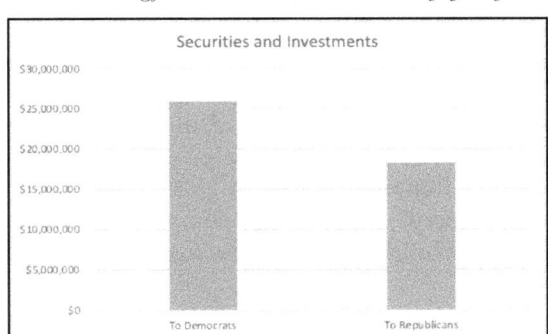

Figure 32: Political Funding from Securities and Investments Industry by Party in 2020

SOURCE: Opensecrets.org
(Securities & Investment Summary 2021)

However, breaking it down by political groups, it's the opposite. Security and Investment companies donated $186.8 million to liberal groups and $217.8 million to conservative groups.

Figure 33 Political Funding from Securities and Investments Industry by Political Groups in 2020

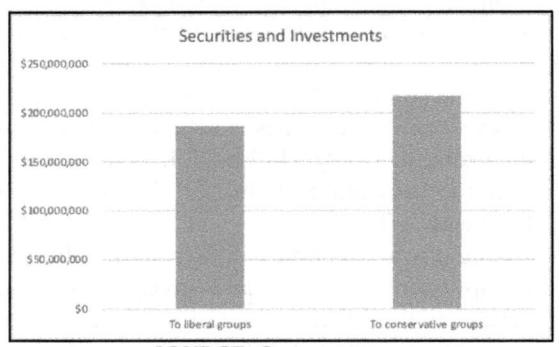

Securities and Investments

[Bar chart: "To liberal groups" approximately $180,000,000; "To conservative groups" approximately $215,000,000]

SOURCE: Opensecrets.org
(Securities & Investment Summary 2021)

While this isn't the only industry that donates a similar amount to Democrats and Republicans, there are comparatively very few. However, the few that they share are normally the industries that get the most negative attention. As an example, out of the top 20 industries in political contributions, only Security/Investment companies, Retired Individuals (Yes, individuals. People who are retired), Real Estate companies, and Insurance companies donate similar amounts to Democrats and Republicans.

Contrary to popular belief, the math shows they're much more different than they are similar. Breaking down all industries for the 2020 election cycle and sorting them by percentages, here are the 20 industries that donated the highest percentage to each party. Of course, this doesn't include organizations specifically created to donate to political candidates or groups.

SOURCE: Opensecrets.org
(Industry Breakdown n.d.)

Industries with the highest percentage of donations to

Democrats:
1. Gun Control | 98.62%
2. LGBTQIA Rights & Issues | 98.49%
3. Pro-Abortion | 98.44%
4. Teachers Unions | 98.17%
5. Unions (Miscellaneous) | 97.15%
6. Environment | 96.68%
7. Industrial Unions | 96.41%
8. Human Rights | 89.76%
9. Public Sector Unions | 88.17%
10. Labor | 87.21%
11. Building Trade Unions | 86.24%
12. Clergy & Religious Organizations | 81.75%
13. Foreign & Defense Policy | 80.65%
14. US Postal Service Unions & Associations | 79.63%
15. Marijuana | 79.21%
16. Transportation Unions | 76.53%
18. Women's Issues | 69.88%
19. Advertising & public relations services | 68.75%
20. Motion Picture production and distribution | 64.56%

Industries with the highest percentage of donations to Republicans:
1. Anti-Abortion | 99.24%
2. Coal Mining | 98.26%
3. Gun Rights | 98.13%
4. Auto Dealers, Foreign Imports | 89%
5. Mining | 86.15%
6. Oil & Gas | 82.13%
7. General Contractors | 80.55%
8. Correctional Facilities Construction & Management | 79.27%
9. Livestock | 78.19%
10. Farm Bureaus | 77.09%
11. Restaurants & Drinking Establishments | 76.74%
12. Business Associations | 75.83%

13. Tobacco | 75.61%
14. Auto Dealers | 72.76%
15. Home Builders | 72.6%
16. Clothing & Accessories | 72.1%
17. Food & Beverage | 71.72%
18. Natural Gas Transmission & Distribution | 71.45%
19. Poultry & Eggs | 71.37%
20. Meat Processing | 70.59%

Long story short, if you don't know much about your local, state, or congressional candidates but you still want your vote to count this coming November, this is an easy way to vote on party lines while simultaneously voting based on the issues that you care most about.

Suffice it to say, when you look at these metrics it becomes very clear. Democrats and Republicans are not funded by the same people.

Legislation by Democrats vs. Republicans

"Democrats and Republicans all vote for the same bills!"

All right, let's look at that as well. I've compiled the votes for major bills during the 118th, 117th, and 116th Congress and analyzed the votes for each of the 435 seats in the House of Representatives. These bills cover immigration policy, foreign affairs, abortion policy, Medicaid and Healthcare policy, climate policy, and taxation. All these bills were voted on by the representatives who, at least partly, received the funding from the 2020 election cycle that we covered in the last chapter.

Let's start with bills from the Energy and Commerce Committee. This committee is responsible for public health, consumer protection, food safety, drug safety, environmental quality, etc. (About n.d.)

The first bill we'll examine from this committee is H.R. 7176, the Unlocking our Domestic LNG Potential Act of 2024. This bill was introduced by Republican August Pfluger, in the 11th District of Texas. Here's the summary of the bill from Congress.gov:

"This bill repeals certain restrictions on the import and export of natural gas under the Natural Gas Act, including requirements for Department of Energy (DOE) approval and related provisions that address free trade agreements. In addition, the bill grants the Federal Energy Regulatory Commission (FERC) the exclusive authority to approve or deny applications to authorize the siting, construction, expansion, or operation of facilities (e.g., liquefied natural gas terminals) to export natural gas to foreign countries or import natural gas from foreign countries. (Currently, DOE authorizes the export or import of natural gas, and FERC authorizes related facilities.)"

In short, the bill removes natural gas restrictions and removes requirements for government approval. If you want to read more, the full text of this bill and all others in this chapter are on Congress.gov. There is also a link in the bibliography section of the book. (H.R.7176 - Unlocking our Domestic LNG Potential Act of 2024 2024)

How did this bill do? Well, at the time of writing it has not been called to vote in the Senate, but it passed the House with 224 votes for the bill and 200 against. The makeup of the votes was on party lines. 96% of the votes for the bill were by Republican voters. Only 9 Democrats voted in favor of the bill, compared to 215 Republicans. 100% of the votes against the bill were from Democratic representatives.

Figure 34: Voting in Favor of Unlocking our Domestic LNG Potential Act by Party

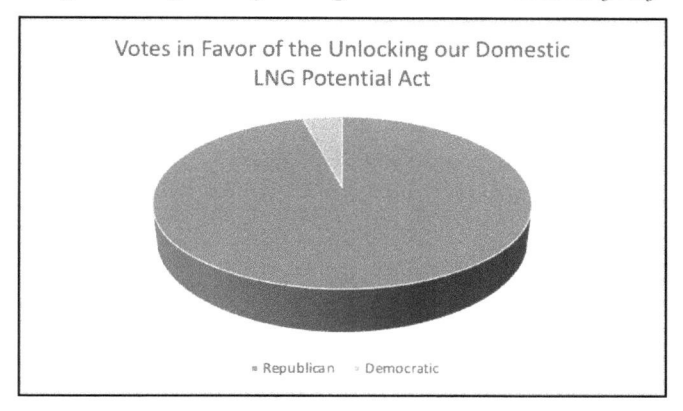

Votes in Favor of the Unlocking our Domestic LNG Potential Act

■ Republican   ■ Democratic

Let's move on to another Energy and Commerce bill, H.R. 7688 - Consumer Fuel Price Gouging Prevention Act. (H.R.7688 - Consumer Fuel Price Gouging Prevention Act 2022) This bill was introduced by Democrat Kim Schrier from the 8th District of Washington. Here's an excerpt of the summary:

"This bill prohibits any person from selling, during a proclaimed energy emergency, a consumer fuel at a price that (1) is unconscionably excessive, and (2) indicates that the seller is exploiting the emergency to increase prices unreasonably. The President may issue a proclamation of such an emergency that specifies the consumer fuel and geographic area covered and how long the proclamation applies."

Let's look at the votes. While at the time of writing, this bill is waiting for legislative action in the Senate, the House passed it with a vote of 217 to 207, again on party lines. This time, it went the opposite way. Out of the votes in favor of the bill, 217 were Democrats. Out of the 207 votes against the bill, 203 were Republican and 4 were Democrats.

Figure 35: Figure 36: Voting in Favor of the Consumer Fuel Price Gouging Prevention Act by Party

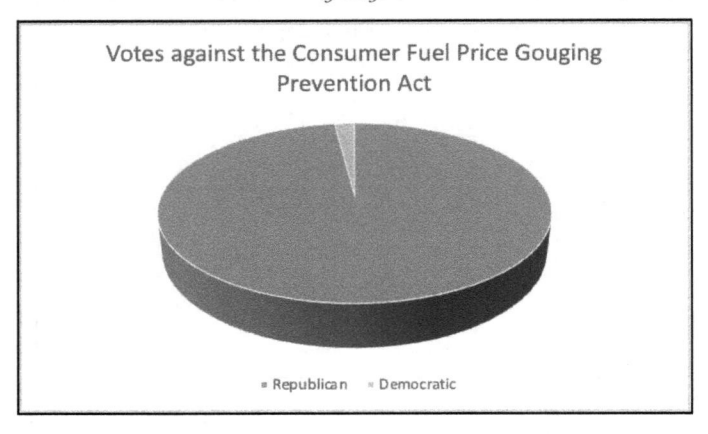

Votes against the Consumer Fuel Price Gouging Prevention Act

- Republican
- Democratic

So, looking at those two bills, Republicans have unanimously voted for fewer restrictions on natural gas companies and allowing fuel companies to price gouge. Democrats have taken the opposite stance, voting nearly unanimously to keep restrictions on natural gas companies and create legislation to stop fuel companies from artificially increasing prices of gas during an emergency.

Let's move on to another committee altogether—the Budget Committee. Led by Republican Chairman Jodey Arrington from the 19th District of Texas, (Members n.d.)this is the committee that brought us the American Rescue Plan Act of 2021.

This bill was one of the first federal responses to the COVID-19 pandemic and was aimed to provide relief to individuals, businesses, and the economy. (H.R.1319 - American Rescue Plan Act of 2021 2021)

Here's an excerpt of the summary:

Specifically, USDA must use specified amounts to

- *provide outreach, mediation, training, and assistance on issues concerning food, agriculture, agricultural credit,*

> agricultural extension, rural development, or nutrition to certain socially disadvantaged groups, including socially disadvantaged farmers, ranchers, or forest landowners;
> - *provide grants and loans to improve land access for such groups;*
> - *fund one or more equity commissions to address racial equity issues within USDA and its programs;*
> - *support and supplement agricultural research, education, and extension, as well as scholarships and programs that provide internships and pathways to federal employment; and*
> - *provide financial assistance to socially disadvantaged farmers, ranchers, or forest landowners who are former farm loan borrowers and suffered related adverse actions or past discrimination or bias in USDA programs.*

Since this bill was reviewed by a Republican-led committee, you'd be forgiven to believe this bill was a Republican-led effort, or at the very least that it was bipartisan. After all, it supported farmers, ranchers, and other organizations that primarily donated to Republicans. Republicans should absolutely have supported this bill, right?

Nope. You'd be wrong. This bill passed on party lines. Not only that, but it barely passed at all with 220 votes for the bill and 211 votes against it.

Out of all 220 votes for the bill, 100% were from Democratic representatives. Out of all 211 votes against the bill, 210 were from Republicans and only one was from a Democrat.

But, unlike the previous bills I've mentioned, this bill was given back to the House after passing the Senate. How did it fare in the Senate?

Well, a very similar situation happened. It passed by a vote of 50 for the bill and 49 against. (Roll Call Vote 117th Congress - 1st Session 2021) All 50 Democrat and Independent Senators voted for the bill and 49 of 50 Republican senators voted for it. What happened to that last

Republican? Dan Sullivan of Alaska didn't vote, so it was sent to the House, then to the president, and was eventually signed into law because of a single vote.

Moving on to another surprising one—the For the People Act of 2021. (H.R.1 - For the People Act of 2021 2021)

This bill was introduced by John P. Sarbanes, a Democrat from Maryland. It went through several committees, including the Intelligence Committee, the Judiciary Committee, the Oversight and Reform Committee, the Science, Space, and Technology Committee, the Education and Labor Committee, the Way and Means Committee, and even a few others. This bill was packed full of legislation and it had an enormous list of goals. Long story short, it makes voting more accessible, it makes voter fraud easier to track, restricts gerrymandering, and it makes money in politics a little more transparent.

Here's an excerpt from the summary:

This bill addresses voter access, election integrity and security, campaign finance, and ethics for the three branches of government.

Specifically, the bill expands voter registration (e.g., automatic and same-day registration) and voting access (e.g., vote-by-mail and early voting). It also limits removing voters from voter rolls.

The bill requires states to establish independent redistricting commissions to carry out congressional redistricting.

Additionally, the bill sets forth provisions related to election security, including sharing intelligence information with state election officials, supporting states in securing their election systems, developing a national strategy to protect U.S. democratic institutions, establishing in the legislative branch the National Commission to Protect United States Democratic Institutions, and other provisions to improve the cybersecurity of election systems.

Further, the bill addresses campaign finance, including expanding the prohibition on campaign spending by foreign nationals, requiring additional disclosure of campaign-related fundraising and spending, requiring additional disclaimers regarding certain political advertising, and establishing an alternative campaign funding system for certain federal offices.

The bill addresses ethics in all three branches of government, including by requiring a code of conduct for Supreme Court Justices, prohibiting Members of the House from serving on the board of a for-profit entity, and establishing additional conflict-of-interest and ethics provisions for federal employees and the White House.

That's a mouthful, right?

It seems like a win-win for voters. How did it do? At the time of writing, there is still no action in the Senate but it did pass the House of Representatives with a vote of 220 to 210. Do you want to guess how both parties voted?

All 220 votes for the bill came from Democratic candidates. Out of the 210 votes against the bill, 209 were Republicans and only 1 was Democratic.

Oh, did you want a pie chart for this one too? Here you go:

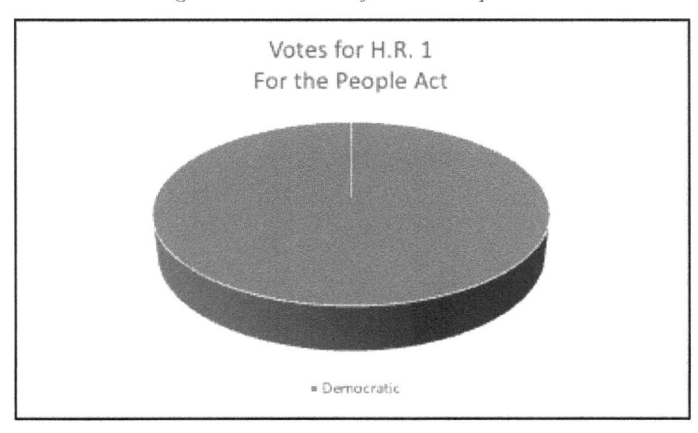

Figure 37: Votes in Favor of the For the People Act

Figure 38: Votes Against the For the People Act

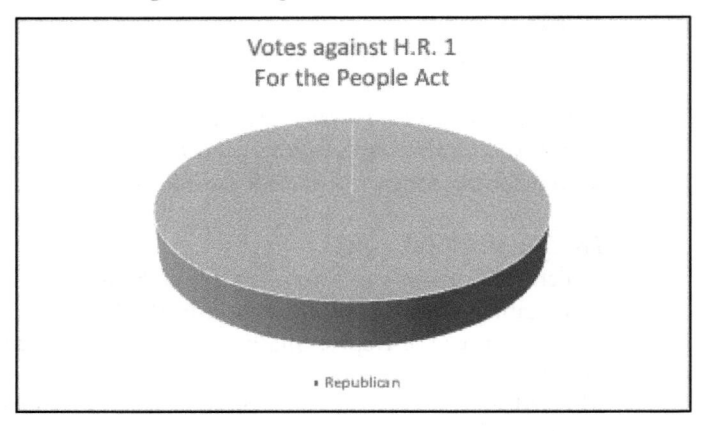

Votes against H.R. 1 For the People Act

• Republican

You're welcome.

Let's do one more. How about H.R. 3684 - the Infrastructure Investment and Jobs Act?

This bill was reviewed by the Transportation and Infrastructure Committee and eventually was signed by President Biden. This, like H.R. 1 is a massive bill with a mind-boggling amount of legislation. Here's an excerpt from the summary:

Among other provisions, this bill provides new funding for infrastructure projects, including for

roads, bridges, and major projects;
passenger and freight rail;
highway and pedestrian safety;
public transit;
broadband;
ports and waterways;
airports;
water infrastructure;
power and grid reliability and resiliency;
resiliency, including funding for coastal resiliency, ecosystem

restoration, and weatherization;
  clean school buses and ferries;
  electric vehicle charging;
  addressing legacy pollution by cleaning up Brownfield and Superfund sites and reclaiming abandoned mines; and
  Western Water Infrastructure.

You can tell where I'm going with this, right? Well, as you may have guessed this bill passed in the Senate with a vote of 69 to 30. 100% of Democratic and Independent Senators voted in favor of the bill, but surprisingly 19 Republicans joined them. However, the remaining 30 Republican Senators voted against the bill. (Roll Call Vote 117th Congress - 1st Session 2021)

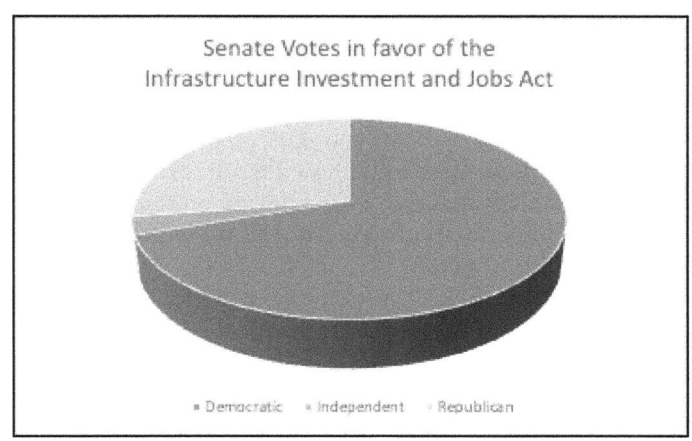

Figure 39: Senate Votes in Favor of the Infrastructure Investment and Jobs Act

Examining the Republican votes specifically, the party was very split. 61% of Republican senators elected to vote for the bill, but 39% voted against it.

Figure 40: Senate Republican Votes in Favor and Against the Infrastructure Investment and Jobs Act

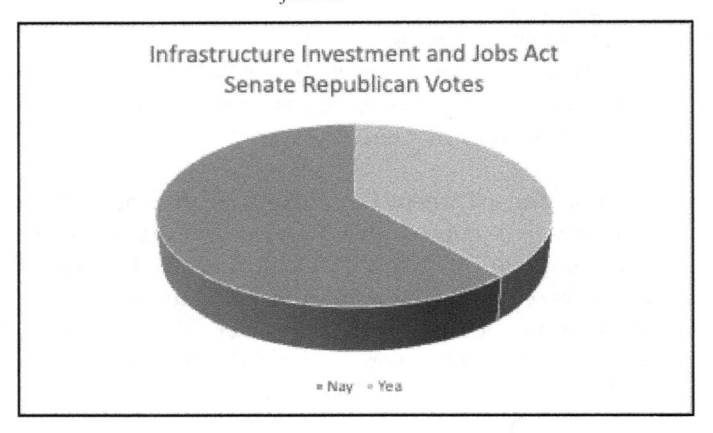

[Pie chart: Infrastructure Investment and Jobs Act Senate Republican Votes — Nay, Yea]

When the bill returned to the house and the motion was made to reconsider, the bill was passed predictably on party lines with 220 Democrats and 8 Republicans voting in favor, and 205 Republicans voting against.

You don't get your chart for those two.

"Yes, yes," I hear you saying. "We've covered this already. All of these bills show that they're different! What about the bills that they vote similarly on? Since Democrats and Republicans both receive AIPAC money, what about those kinds of bills?"

All right, all right. Let's move to H.R. 7217 - the Israel Security Supplemental Appropriations Act of 2024. (H.R.7217 - Israel Security Supplemental Appropriations Act, 2024 2024) This was a bill that provided appropriations for Israel's retaliation against the Hamas terrorist attack. The bill was introduced by Republican Ken Calvert in the 41st District of California in February of 2024, during the time in which word was spreading about Israel's attack on the Gaza Strip. Here's an excerpt of the summary from Congress.gov:

This bill provides FY2024 supplemental appropriations to the

Department of Defense (DOD) and the Department of State for activities to respond to the attacks in Israel. The bill designates the funding as emergency spending, which is exempt from discretionary spending limits.

Specifically, the bill provides appropriations to DOD for

- *Military Personnel;*
- *Operation and Maintenance;*
- *Procurement;*
- *Research, Development, Test and Evaluation;*
- *Defense Working Capital Funds; and*
- *the Defense Health Program.*
- *The funding is provided for purposes such as*
- *supporting current U.S. military operations in the region;*
- *replacing defense articles that were provided to Israel;*
- *reimbursing DOD for defense services and training provided to Israel; and*
- *procuring Israel's Iron Dome, David's Sling, and Iron Beam defense systems to counter short-range rocket threats.*
- *The bill also provides appropriations to the State Department for*
- *Diplomatic Programs,*
- *Emergencies in the Diplomatic and Consular Service, and*
- *the Foreign Military Financing Program.*

It needed two-thirds vote in the house and it failed with 250 votes for and 180 votes against.

Out of all the votes in favor of the bill, 204 of them, or 82% were Republican votes. Only 46 Democrats voted for the bill, meaning Democrats made up less than 19% of the "yea" votes.

Figure 41: Votes in Favor of the Israel Security Supplemental Appropriations Act

[Pie chart: Votes in Favor of the Israel Security Supplemental Appropriations Act — Republican, Democratic]

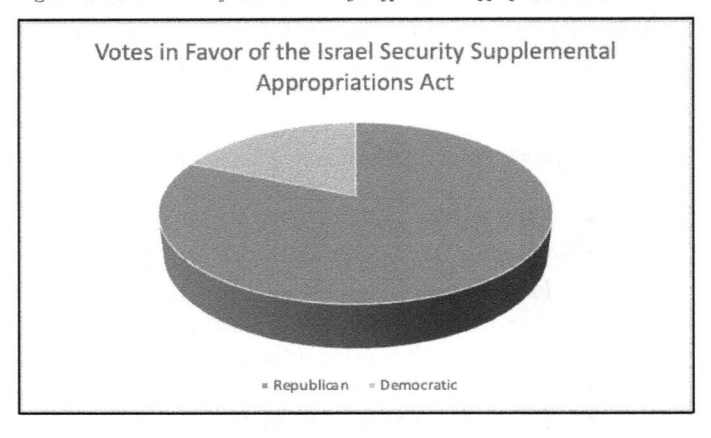

The difference between the two parties is even more drastic when you look at the votes against the bill. Out of all the 180 "nay" votes, 166, or 92% of them were from Democrats. The remaining 14, or 8% were from Republicans.

Figure 42: Votes Against the Israel Security Supplemental Appropriations Act

[Pie chart: Votes against the Israel Security Supplemental Appropriations Act — Democratic, Republican]

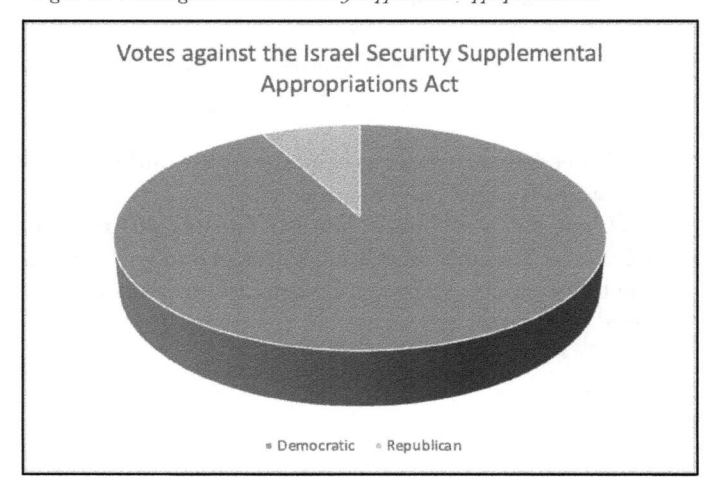

So, while it's a common belief that both parties unanimously support Israel and tangentially unanimously support Israel's attack on Gaza, that belief does not hold true in practice. Throughout Israel's response in Palestine, many Democrats have voted against assisting them.

All right, well what about the TikTok ban? Yes, this is another fantastic example. Let's talk about H.R. 7521, one of the most infamous bills put forth by the current Congress. This bill was introduced by Republican Mike Gallagher in the 8th District of Wisconsin. At the time of writing, this bill has yet to be voted on in the Senate.

Here's an excerpt of the summary from Congress.gov:

This bill prohibits distributing, maintaining, or providing internet hosting services for a foreign adversary-controlled application (e.g., TikTok). However, the prohibition does not apply to a covered application that executes a qualified divestiture as determined by the President.

Under the bill, a foreign adversary-controlled application is directly or indirectly operated by (1) ByteDance, Ltd. or TikTok (including subsidiaries or successors that are controlled by a foreign adversary); or (2) a social media company that is controlled by a foreign adversary and has been determined by the President to present a significant threat to national security. The prohibition does not apply to an application that is primarily used to post product reviews, business reviews, or travel information and reviews.

As many others have said, the text of this bill is extremely problematic and very vague. However, one thing that's universally agreed upon is that it's designed to force a sale or ban of TikTok in the United States.

Unlike the other bills mentioned in this chapter, H.R. 7521 is much more bipartisan. Only 65 House representatives voted against this bill, while 352 voted for the bill. Out of those 352 who voted in favor of the bill, 197 or 56% were Republicans. 155, or 44% were Democrats.

Figure 43: Votes in Favor of the Protecting Americans from Foreign Adversary Controlled Applications Act

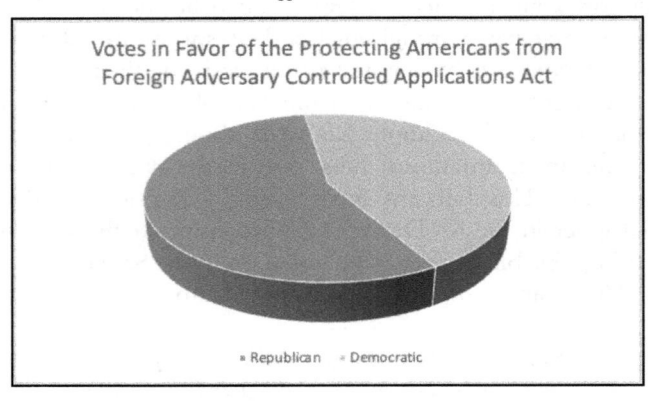

As a result, yes. This was a bipartisan bill. However, that still does not mean that these two parties are the same. When you look at the votes against the bill, it paints a much different picture. Out of the 65 "nays" 50 of those, or 77% were from Democratic representatives, whereas only 15 Republicans voted no.

Figure 44: Votes in Favor of the Protecting Americans from Foreign Adversary Controlled Applications Act

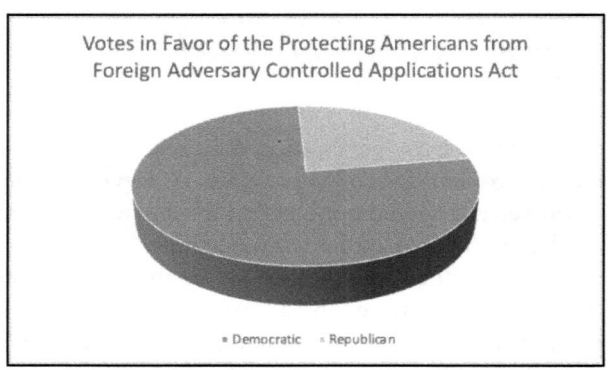

So, all told, while this bill was bipartisan, that doesn't

mean that both parties reacted to it the same way. While the majority of both parties agreed with the bill, the Republican party was much more monolithic. Out of the 212 Republicans who voted "Yea" or "Nay", 197 voted to pass the bill. Meaning, the bill had the support of 93% of the Republicans who voted.

Figure 45: Protecting Americans from Foreign Adversary Controlled Applications Act Republican Votes

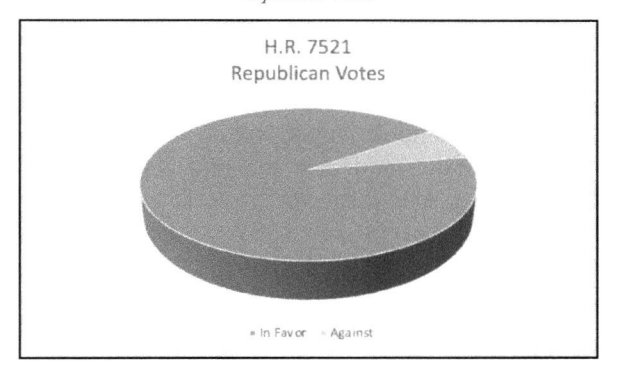

On the Democratic side, things look a little different. Out of the 205 Democrats who voted one way or another, 155 of them, or 76% voted for the bill.

Figure 46: Protecting Americans from Foreign Adversary Controlled Applications Act Democrat Votes

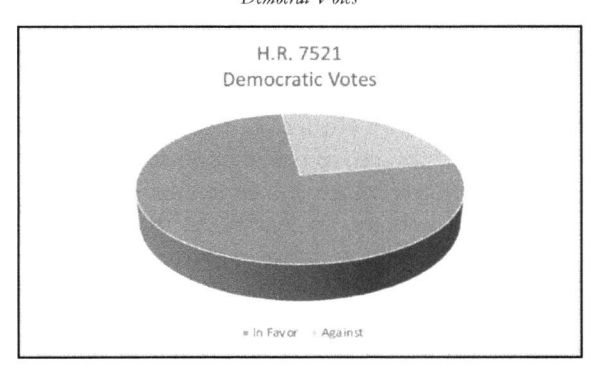

So, all told, while only 7% of Republicans were against the bill, 24% of Democrats were against it. While that's the smallest difference out of nearly all major pieces of legislation in the last 10 years, the differences are still very visible.

If you're basing your vote this coming November on this one issue, the numbers are easy to see. While both parties have a large selection of candidates who support banning TikTok, if you're against the ban or forced sale, there is only one political party in which candidates have the potential to vote in your favor, and that's the Democratic Party.

But all told, it's safe to say that when comparing both parties, even if you don't align politically with either one, it's important to understand that the impacts of legislation, political funding, and local and state laws are drastically different in both parties. Even if you dislike both parties equally, the claim that both parties are the same is categorically and demonstratively false.

If you want to claim that both parties are secretly in cahoots or there is some underlying puppet master who's orchestrating this entire thing, these kinds of claims need remarkable evidence. This evidence would not just have to be more substantive than the evidence brought against it, but it would also have to explain the fact that Democrats and Republicans are funded by vastly different interest groups, vote extremely differently on national legislation, and have completely different statistics surrounding state and local data when one party overwhelmingly controls that area's political landscape.

The claim that both parties are bad, or equally bad is a profoundly difficult claim to prove because the fact is, all of our evidence, from voting records to financial records, to speeches and to debates, to legislation they introduce, to their recorded hearings in congress all point to the same fact—Democrats and Republicans are two politically opposed parties. They have fundamentally different views of how the country should operate, and the outcomes of

those views are measurable and easily identifiable.
    The major parties are NOT the same.
    Are we stuck with them?

Voting Third Party

"I'm just going to vote for a third-party candidate!"

First and foremost, I want to make it very clear that I'm not telling you to vote for any candidate or any party. The goal of this message is to encourage you to think about which one of the two main candidates in the general election you'd prefer if you were forced to choose one, then I'd like you to understand the consequences of voting for that party.

I've covered the differences between the two major parties and candidates pretty extensively, so let's get into what it means to vote for a third party in the United States and what outcomes that can have.

The first important topic is the history of political parties in the United States. Specifically, the fact that every single political party in the history of the United States has come about either by a merging of existing parties, splitting a party that has a stronghold, or from an existing party collapsing and reemerging as a different party.

Throughout our entire history, that has been true with every major political party. Most importantly, in our entire history, there has never been a point in time where there were three successful presidential parties that existed simultaneously.

This is not only due to the lack of popularity that a third party inevitably faces, it's also not just due to voters refusing to risk their vote, and it's not just due to the lack of viable candidates, although all three of those problems absolutely play into it. Even if these problems didn't exist, we still wouldn't be able to get a major third party, or even to get a candidate from that party elected.

Why? Because of the way that the Electoral College works, which we will address in just a little bit.

But first, let's talk briefly about the history of our political parties and how our current political parties came to be.

The Republican Party came from the Whig Party which came from the National Republican Party. (History.com Editors 2021) The National Republican Party is what split the Democrats and the Republicans from the Democratic-Republican Party, which was known then as the Republican Party. Before then, the Democratic-Republican Party faced against the Federalist Party and before those two parties, there were no political parties active during presidential elections.

All political parties have been a natural evolution of other political parties since the birth of the United States. That context is extremely important if we plan to form and vote for a viable third party because there are only two routes that have been proven to be historically successful.

The first one is to replace one of the parties that we currently have with another party. In other words, you have to vote for one party consistently for several presidential elections, several statewide elections, *and* several Congressional elections so that the other party dies out. This is what happened to the Federalists. This is also what happened to the National Republican Party. This is also what happened to the Whig party.

Once the opposing party dies out, the remaining party will need to split and become two separate parties. This is what happened with the Democratic-Republican Party, back then called the Republican Party, when it forked into the National Republican Party and the Democratic Party.

If we truly want another political party and we want that political party to be successful, the only way to do that with our current system is to eliminate one of the parties and allow the remaining party to split into smaller versions of that party. If we stop voting for the Democrats, then the Democrats are the ones getting the axe.

It won't likely be a brand new party that rises up to replace it, either. It will be the remaining party, the Republican party, splitting into two separate Republican parties after rising into power for many, many elections.

If your goal is to oppose the Democrats, if history is replicated, there are two likely outcomes:

First, it could split the Republican party,—which means issues such as gay and interracial marriage, abortion legality, government assistance, etc., would all be universally agreed on by both political parties.

On the other hand, the Democratic Party might resurface as a new party. However, if this happens, the party that replaces the Democrats would lean more conservative than they do currently, in hopes of winning over Republican voters.

Either way, if the Democratic Party were to collapse the only difference between the Republican Party and the brand new party would be the differences Republican candidates already have amongst each other.

The same principle holds true if the Republican party collapses. If your goal is to oppose the Republicans and the

Republican party collapses, the party that replaces them would either be a rebirth of the current Republican Party with slightly different views, or a split in the Democratic Party.

However, if your goal is to get a progressive or leftist political party in the United States, the most likely means is for the Republican party to collapse and the Democratic Party to split. If the Democrats remain in power for several elections and split, it would likely be on political lines already drawn by the current Democratic candidates. This means we'd have a moderate/liberal Democratic party consisting of candidates with similar values to Joe Biden or Hillary Clinton, etc. Then, we'd have a progressive/leftist Democratic party consisting of candidates with similar views to Bernie Sanders and Alexandria Ocasio-Cortez.

So, if you're anti-racism, anti-sexism, anti-voter suppression, you believe that women have a right to their own bodies, et cetera, you probably don't want the Democratic Party to fail.

The good news, however, is that Republicans have lost the popular vote in every first-time presidential election since 1988. In fact, the only time a Republican has won the popular vote in a presidential election in 36 years was George W. Bush's re-election in 2004—an election that occurred 20 years ago.

Fun fact: 25.17% of the United States population is under 20 years old, which means over a **quarter of our country's population was born after the last time a Republican won the popular vote.** (Neilsberg Research 2023)

Support for the Republican Party is dwindling. Currently, the Republicans are doing so poorly that they have to rely on the electoral college to win the presidency, have to rely on gerrymandering to win the house votes, and have to rely on voter suppression to win state elections and senate elections. If we keep doing the same thing that we did in 2020 and 2022, then the Republican Party will eventually collapse and we will get that third party.

Another fun fact: The last non-incumbent Republican president to get the popular vote was in 1988, **which means nearly half of the population has not seen a first-time Republican win the popular vote within their lifetime.**

But I know what you're thinking. You don't want to continue voting for the Democrats. That's fair. How do we get another third party without voting for the Democrats?

Well, in our current system, we can't.

I'm not saying it's unlikely, I'm saying mathematically it's so improbable that it's a safe assumption that it will never happen until our system is changed.

So why can't it happen?

Why can't the United States have three concurrent parties? Was it an elaborate plan by the founding fathers to eliminate all representation from candidates who don't have generational wealth? Is there some conspiracy that intentionally creates exclusionary outcomes? Is there something in the constitution that makes it illegal or something?

No. It may seem ludicrous, but there are no political reasons behind this. It's not some insidious plan set forth by politicians of old and enforced by those in power today. The truth is much, much more frustrating. It all comes down to mathematics.

In the United States, we use a system called the Electoral College, which is a winner-take-all system broken down by state. When a presidential candidate wins the election in a state, they are given a number of electoral points which are determined by population. However, since this is a winner-take-all system, it makes it very difficult for more than two candidates to have any representation. In fact, there have been many situations when it stops more than one candidate from having any representation at all.

Here are a few examples of how this works.

Let's say we're conducting an election and squares represent people.

Since this is in book form, let's say there are two colors, light gray and dark gray. There are thirty squares total, 12 of which are light and 18 are dark.

Figure 47: A Grid of Electoral Squares

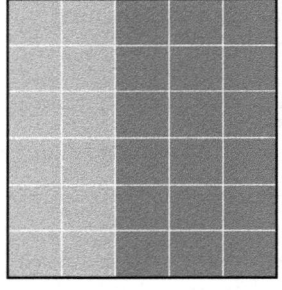

Dark wins, right?

Well, with the Electoral College, we don't measure the total number of squares, we measure it by area. Areas can be of many sizes and can contain any amount of light and dark squares.

Take a look at this example:

Figure 48: Election Grid Divided by Districts

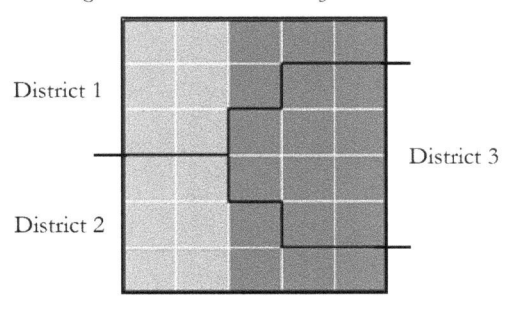

Table 1: Election Grid District Totals

Name	Light	Dark	Winner
District 1	6	4	Light
District 2	0	10	Dark
District 3	6	4	Light

Even though all three districts in this chart have the same number of squares, the results are not the same as the total. Districts 1 and 3 have 4 dark squares and six light squares, while district 2 has 10 dark squares and no light squares.

In this example, light would win even though more people voted for dark.

But, while this is already unfair, the states within Electoral College don't have same population. As a result, what often happens is something that looks like this:

Figure 49: Election Grid Divided by 6 Districts

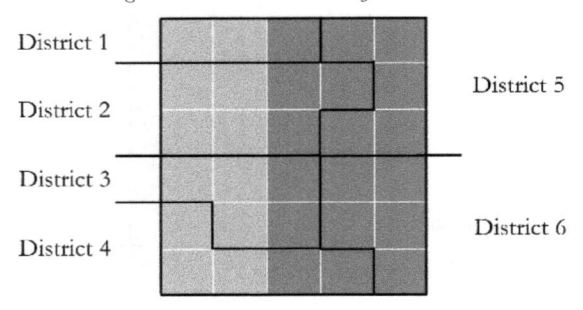

In this example, we have districts of many sizes, from as small as 3 to as large as 7. Because of the location of the districts, light wins by an even greater amount than in the last example. Out of six districts, light only wins two of them.

However, you may have noticed, states in the electoral college are not all equal in point value. Instead, the electoral college points are based on the population of each state. Does that make it fairer? Let's take a look.

Table 2: Election Grid with 6 Districts and Totals

Name	Light	Dark	Winner	Light Points	Dark Points
District 1	2	1	Light	3	0
District 2	4	3	Light	7	0
District 3	3	2	Light	5	0
District 4	3	2	Light	5	0
District 5	0	5	Dark	0	5
District 6	0	5	Dark	0	5
Total	12	18	Light	20	10

As it turns out, even when we factor in population, dark will still lose every election and it's not even close. In this example, dark only earned 10 electoral points, while light earned 20. If this were an actual election, light would have a much better chance of winning. However, that victory isn't guaranteed.

In fact, the entire election still comes down to one of two squares. These two squares are the most important in the entire election.

Which ones?

The two light squares that touch the dark area in District 2. If just one of those squares flip dark, the entire election changes and is now won by the dark squares.

Figure 50: Election Grid Divided by 6 Districts - Adjusted Vote in District 2

Table 3: Election Grid Divided by 6 Districts and Totals – Adjusted Vote in District 2

Name	Light	Dark	Winner	Light Points	Dark Points
District 1	2	1	Light	3	0
District 2	3	4	Dark	0	7
District 3	3	2	Light	5	0
District 4	3	2	Light	5	0
District 5	0	5	Dark	0	5
District 6	0	5	Dark	0	5
Total	11	19	Light	13	17

Fun fact, this is exactly what happened in Florida during Election 2000. Or, more accurately, *what almost happened.*

How does this work?

Long story short, it's because of the winner-take-all system. When a color wins a district, no matter the ratio, it's as if everyone in that district voted for that color. When a candidate loses a district that has very few of their voters, it's not as big of a deal of losing a district that has a lot of their voters.

Let's look at District 1 as an example. District 1 has 2 light votes and 1 dark vote. If light wins District 1, they pick up the value of a dark vote. That's great, but it's not as big of an impact as District 2. If light wins District 2, they pick up 3 additional votes. However, if they lose District 2, they give dark 3 additional votes.

As a result, in all these situations, the election is not a reflection of the population. It's not just a battle of earning votes, but also a battle to see how many of the oppositions votes you can take when your state wins.

But Nick, what does this have to do with third parties?

I'm glad you asked. Let's say Jane Q. Public ran in this election as the color white. In this scenario, let's say Jane is popular with those who vote dark, but she is too radical for those who vote light.

No matter which squares Jane takes, if she is not able to take squares away from the light squares, there is no way for her to win.

The only way she would be able to win the election is by winning every single dark district on the board and taking over a white square from District 2.

I'll give you a blank sheet so you can try it out for yourself.

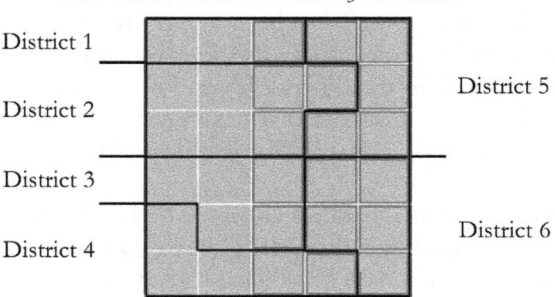

Table 4: Blank Election Grid Divided by Six Districts

However, it's important to note that since Jane would be splitting the vote, it's not likely she'd take most of the dark squares anyway.

But okay, let's say she was so popular that she stole some of the light squares. Let's also say she got the most squares out of all of the candidates.

There are many ways this could happen, but for the sake of education, let's say the election ended up like this:

Figure 51: Election Grid Divided by 6 Districts with Added Third Party

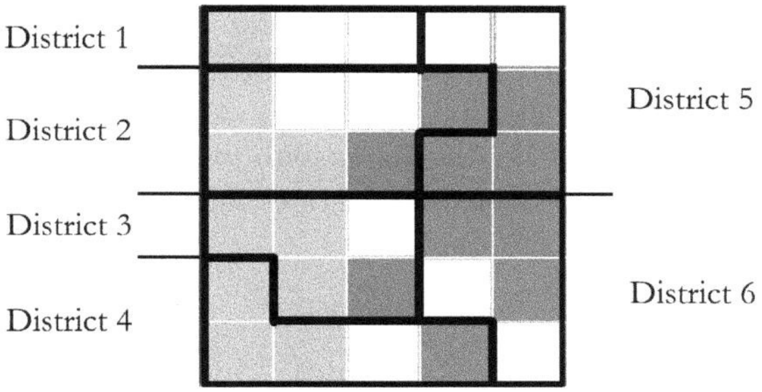

Table 5: Election Grid Divided by 6 Districts with Added Third Party

Name	Light	Dark	White	Winner	Light Points	Dark Points	White Points
District 1	1	0	2	White	0	0	3
District 2	3	2	2	Light	7	0	0
District 3	3	1	1	Light	5	0	0
District 4	3	1	1	Light	5	0	0
District 5	0	3	2	Dark	0	5	0
District 6	0	2	3	White	0	0	5
Total	10	9	11	Light	17	5	8

In this example, Jane had 11 squares, dark had 9 squares and light had 10. However, dark only earned 5 electoral points and white only earned 8. In this situation, light won again with 17 points.

What's worse, is even though Jane got the most squares, because of the math behind districts, she got less than half of the electoral points.

As you can see by this example, the addition of more political parties makes the problem of voter distribution even worse. When light wins a district, even though they win by a small margin every time, the dark and white votes in that District are given to light. If this happens in the majority of districts, light is guaranteed to win. Not because of the amount of votes they earn, but because of the amount of votes they steal.

This is how the Electoral College works, but on a much larger scale. While it's certainly possible for a candidate to win the popular vote and the Electoral College vote, it's just as likely for a candidate to win the election without the popular vote solely because they targeted the right voters.

Now, the most common justification for the Electoral College is the claim that it allows each state to have representation, even the states with the fewest population.

However, look at the grid once again. Does it look like District 1 has representation?

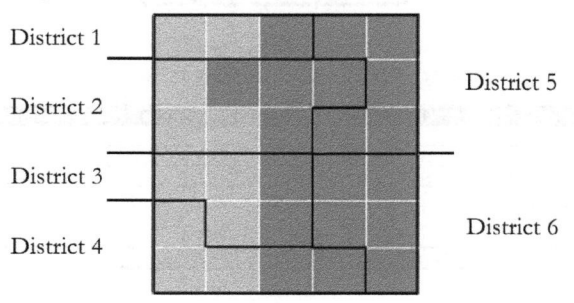

Figure 52: Election Grid Divided by 6 Districts - Adjusted Vote in District 2

Table 6: Election Grid Divided by 6 Districts ant Totals - Adjusted Vote in District 2

Name	Light	Dark	Winner	Light Points	Dark Points
District 1	2	1	Light	3	0
District 2	3	4	Dark	0	7
District 3	3	2	Light	5	0
District 4	3	2	Light	5	0
District 5	0	5	Dark	0	5
District 6	0	5	Dark	0	5
Total	11	19	Light	13	17

If District 1 were to flip dark, the election results would

be the same. In fact, very few of the smaller districts have much say in their votes. If light voters in District 5 decided to push to flip the state, they would have to flip three squares just for their vote to count.

Same with District 6.

It's safe to say that on this board, the voters who have the most representation are the ones from District 2, which is the most populous district. Smaller Districts like 1, 3 and 4 have some representation, however it would take flipping two of those districts to win the election.

All while Districts 5 and 6 have little to no representation. 3 times as many voters would have to switch their vote in Districts 5 and 6 to equal one voter switching in District 1, 3, and 4.

It would also take twice as many voters in Districts 1, 3, and 4 to flip the election as it would in District 2.

Bottom line, there is no evidence to support that the Electoral College gives voters in smaller states more representation than the popular vote. While it may feel like it gives voters representation because smaller states are easier for voters to flip, the impact of that flip is what matters.

In the Electoral College, the impact is all too often negligible.

Let's do some real-world examples.

Nearly every state is winner-take-all or at least have winner-take-all triggers, with two exceptions—Maine and Nebraska—which appoint electors based on district, and then add 2 electors for the candidate that wins the popular vote. (Distribution of Electoral Votes n.d.)

Let's take Election 2020 as an example. To do the math, I took all the votes for each candidate from each state plus Washington D.C. and then created a series of formulas to determine how many votes each candidate would have if various percentages of them switched to a singular third-party candidate.

If you want to see the data yourself, I compiled it all in a spreadsheet which is available on my website for free. If you have Microsoft Excel, you can even use it as a calculator and do some of the match yourself.

The goal of this exercise is to find out what percentage of the population would need to change their votes to a Third-party candidate to allow that candidate to be elected President.

Now, of course, there are a few difficulties with approaching it this way. Firstly, since the 2020 election, the Electoral College has been updated based on populations from the 2020 census, meaning that these Electoral College numbers aren't necessarily 1-to-1 comparisons with future elections. I chose to use the 2020 election because it was the most recent presidential election, as such we can quantify the votes with a greater amount of certainty than what would have if I updated the populations and electoral college for each state since it's not possible to determine the political affiliations of the people who moved from one state to another.

Another problem with this methodology is that in 2020 there were already third-party candidates who received small percentages of the votes—the highest one being Jo Jorgensen with 1.8% of the national vote. These third-party candidates aren't factored into this experiment because the goal of this exercise was to focus all third-party votes on a singular candidate. Add to that, an additional goal of this exercise was to test for the impact of ranked-choice-voting, should it be implemented. Since we can't fully guarantee which candidate these voters would've voted for, I chose to remove them from the calculations altogether. As a result, my estimated margin of error is 2-3% across all of these metrics.

Now, with that out of the way, let's do our first test.

Let's say there is a third-party candidate who is so popular that 30% of voters across the country switched their votes from Democratic to Third Party.

If that happened, according to these projections, it

would've split the Democratic votes so heavily that the Republicans would've won Arizona, Colorado, Georgia, Illinois, Maine, Michigan, Minnesota, New Hampshire, New Jersey, New Mexico, Nebraska, Oregon, Pennsylvania, Virginia, and Wisconsin as well as all the states they won in 2020.

As a result, Donald Trump would win the presidential race with 396 electoral votes, with Joe Biden trailing in at 142.

That's a major difference.

Figure 53:Electoral College Map Simulating a 30% Democratic Switch to Third-Party

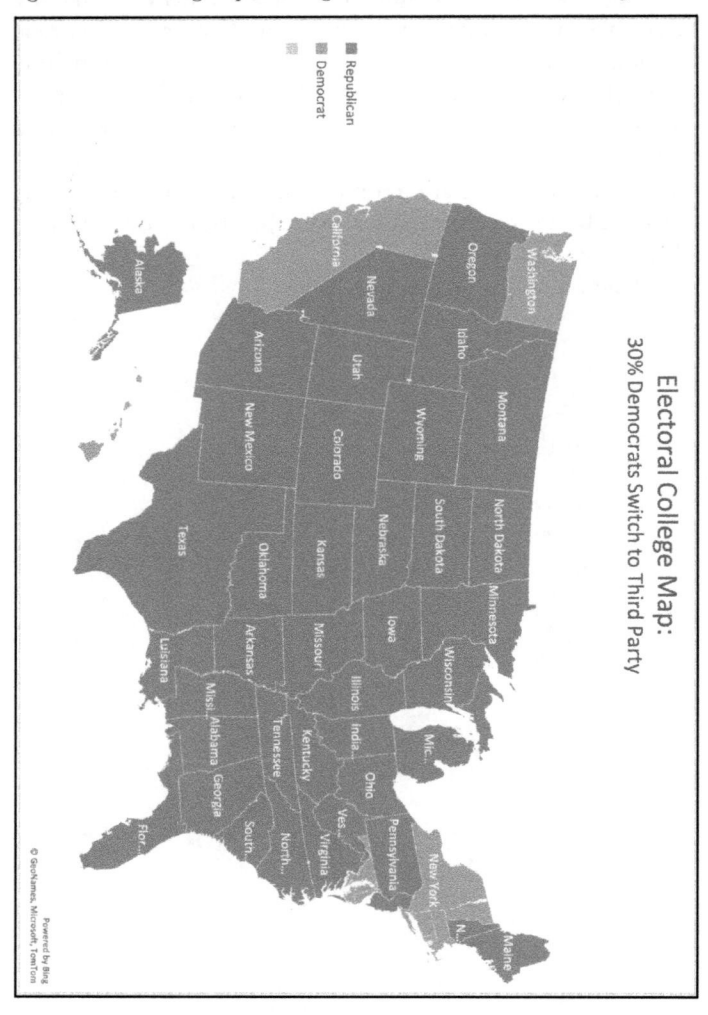

Electoral College Map: 30% Democrats Switch to Third Party

But what if some Republican voters voted for that Third-Party candidate as well? Let's run the numbers with 20% of Republican voters switching over to Third-Party as well as the 30% of Democratic voters.

Figure 54: Electoral College Map Simulating a 30% Democratic Switch and 20% Republican Switch to Third Party

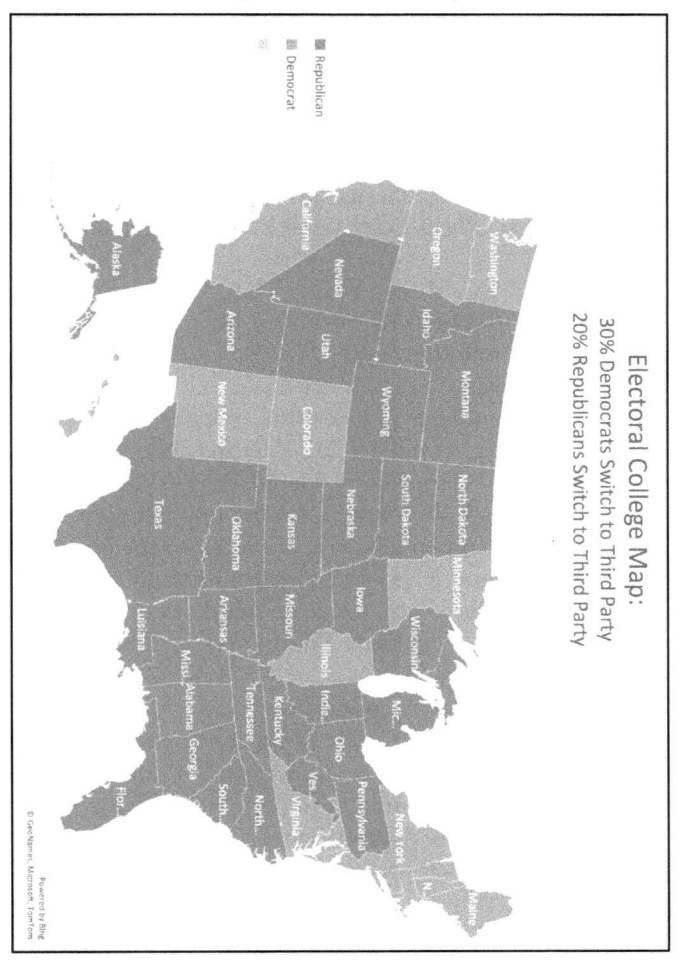

In this case the race is closer, but Donald Trump would still win with 311 electoral votes, Biden comes in second with 227, and the Third-Party candidate still doesn't win a single state.

To put this in perspective for you, let's do one more example but turn the craziness up to 11.

Doing the math, what would happen if 35% of Democrats switched to Third-Party, 30% of Republicans switched to Third-Party, and 5% of the adult population who didn't vote in 2020 voted for Third-Party.

That would be incredible, right? You may be thinking to yourself, "30% of Republicans and 35% of Democrats? Plus the non-voters? Third-Party would have to get the most votes, right?"

Well, yes. You'd be right. That candidate would absolutely win the popular vote. But how many Electoral College votes would they get?

Are you ready?

Joe Biden would get 212 electoral college votes.

Donald Trump would get 232 electoral college votes.

Our champion Third-Party candidate? They would only get 94, even though they would win the popular vote.

What would happen next is it would go to the House of Representatives and it would be voted on there, with one vote per state. However, keep in mind, at the time of writing, there are no current Third-Party members of the House of Representatives.

Hopefully, you see the point now.

The reason we can't have three concurrent political parties in the United States is because of the Electoral College system. If we want a third party, and we don't want to vote for a current political party to get one, the only remaining option is to eliminate or bypass the Electoral College.

Figure 55: Electoral College Map Simulating a 35% Democratic Switch, 30% Republican Switch, and 5% Non-Voter Switch to Third-Party

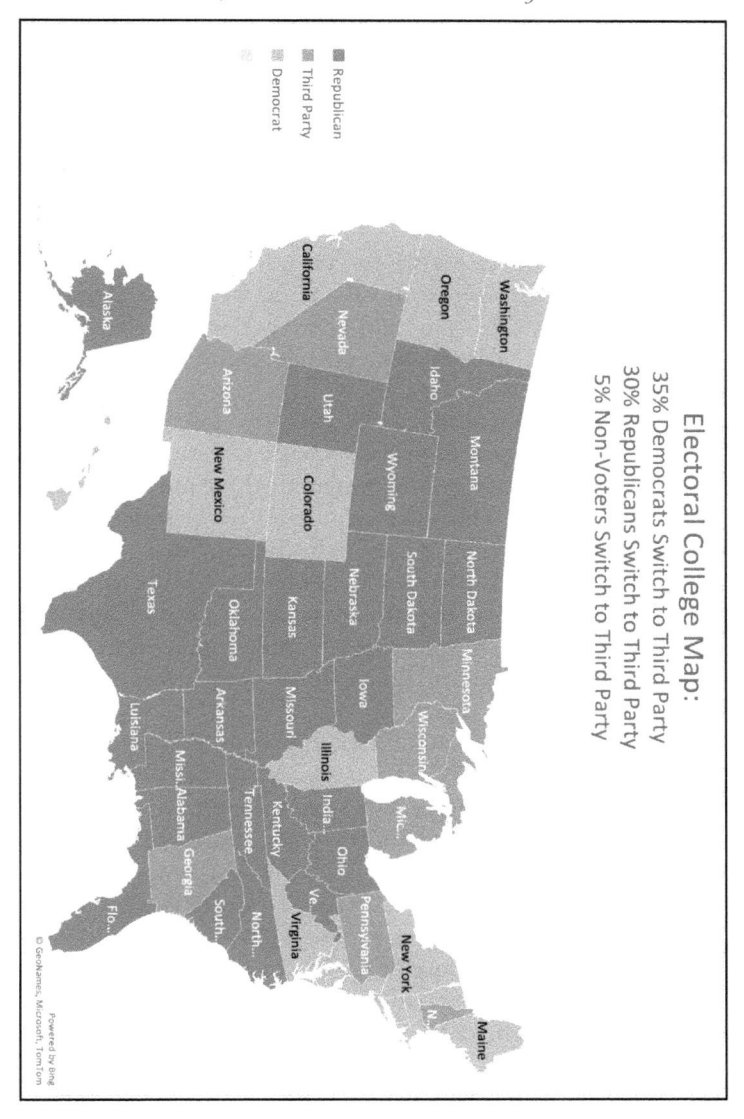

You may be thinking, "This sounds impossible" but don't give up on me now.

There are two options.

The first option would be to elect enough Third-Party candidates in Congress who would be willing to pass a constitutional amendment, or we would have to get enough states to enter the National Popular Vote Interstate Compact. I will further elaborate on these options later in the book.

However, suffice it to say, even if Congress passed an amendment to remove the Electoral College, a president would likely veto the bill anyway because the sitting president was almost certainly elected by the electoral college system to get elected.

If the President does not veto the bill, the Supreme Court may step in and declare it unconstitutional. After all, at the time of writing, there were only three members of the Supreme Court who were appointed by Democrats. The remaining six were appointed by Republicans. (Table of Supreme Court Justices n.d.) Remember earlier when we talked about how the Republicans need the Electoral College system to get elected? It's unlikely that the Supreme Court will side against the political party who appointed them.

As a result, if we decide to take the route of a constitutional amendment, we need to start electing enough candidates into Congress who are willing to eliminate the Electoral College to override a veto, and we also need to continue to elect presidents who will appoint Supreme Court Justices who are unlikely to rule that amendment unconstitutional. In order to do this, we would need two-thirds of both the House of Representatives and the Senate, and we'll need to have had a Democratic president in office for long enough to have appointed two Supreme Court Justices.

The good news is many, many, many Democrats in Congress already support this idea. However, if our goal is to pass a constitutional amendment to eliminate the Electoral College, we will need to start putting the same level of energy and activism into voting for more of these candidates in the House and Senate as we have for the Presidential elections. Not only that, but we need to continue to vote in Presidential Elections for several more cycles.

Since Democrats have been losing to the Electoral College since 1988, it's not a stretch to say that there are Democrats in Congress who will support the idea of eliminating it. We just have to show up to the polls and make sure they're in office.

This is how we get a true third party, not one that replaces another party, not one that is a reincarnation of another party, but an actual concurrent third party in the United States. Eliminating or bypassing the Electoral College is the only way, mathematically, to do that.

"If we all stop voting for Democrats, they're gonna have to get more and more left-leaning in order to survive, right?"

No, not at all.

Historically, that has not been the case. In the election of 2000, we had one of the most progressive candidates in modern history on the ticket, Al Gore. Al Gore was against "Don't Ask, Don't Tell," campaigned on climate-change legislation, was pro-union, etc. (Richter and Brownstein 1999), (Seelye and Greenhouse 1999), (Macilwain 1998)

Was he a leftist? No. He still disagreed with gay marriage, was pro-free trade, etc. But when you compare his policies to other presidential candidates in the last 40 years, he was extremely progressive.

In 2000, he won the popular vote but lost the election because of the Electoral College.

The reason that he lost the votes, contrary to popular opinion isn't because of George W. Bush's popularity, it's because Ralph Nader, and independents, split the vote.

The next election, John Kerry one the Primary, who was even more progressive than Al Gore. He was pro-choice, he was an advocate for separation of church and state, he was pro-gay marriage, he was against assisting large corporations at the cost of citizens and small businesses, etc. (The Associated Press 2004), (The Associated Press 2004)

However, John Kerry lost the election by 35 points. He also lost the popular vote by over 2 million votes.

After these elections, the Democrats realized that if they continued their left-leaning trajectory, they'd continue to lose support for moderate voters. Also, if they lose the support of leftists, those leftists won't turn around and vote Republican. The moderate voters absolutely would.

Add to that, there were (and still are) more moderate voters in the United States than leftists. So, if they moved toward the center they could gain more moderate votes than they would lose from leftists.

This made the moderate voter base twice as valuable, and twice as plentiful as the leftists, therefore they needed to switch their platform and become more moderate.

And that's exactly what they did. They pushed for a more conservative candidate in 2008 and Obama won the Presidency.

It's weird to think about Obama being a conservative, but it's true.

Obama said himself that he was pretty much a conservative candidate from the 1980s, (Swanson 2012) but hey, that's what wins the moderate votes, and that's what won Obama the presidency. Obama stole many more moderate votes from the Republicans than he lost from the leftists.

And in 2016 it happened again. Hillary Clinton ran on

many of Bill Clinton's political stances.

However, she couldn't appeal to enough moderates to win their vote, and pushing a leftist appeal was unlikely to be successful while Jill Stein was running.

As a result, Jill Stein took Clinton's leftist votes and both Clinton and Trump lost moderate votes to Gary Johnson.

Johnson didn't gain enough votes to lose him the election, but he gained enough of Clinton's moderate votes to force her to lose the electoral college.

As a result in 2020, the Democrats ran Biden, who won enough of the moderates and made up for the lost leftist votes.

Long story short, the more we protest vote, the more conservative Democrats become.

Leftists are not only an unreliable voter base but there aren't enough to win elections. Add to that, a single moderate vote is worth two since it takes a vote away from the Republicans.

Democrats who try to win leftist votes lose the election every single time. Protest voting will not encourage Democrats to appeal to progressives, in fact, the opposite tends to happen. The unfortunate truth is the more leftists protest vote, the more likely it will be that both parties move further right.

As a fellow leftist, it's a frustrating and terrifying realization to have, but also as a leftist, I rely on facts and data to form my opinions. Unfortunately, when you look at the facts, the ugly truth is right there in front of us.

We are not reliable. Presidential candidates cannot count on us at the polls. We are not loyal to candidates, political parties, or even our country in general.

Moderates on the other hand are very reliable. Every time the Democrats scoot more conservative, they win the vote. And every time Republicans go a little bit more conservative, they lose the vote.

So… the unfortunate truth is if we want candidates with leftist beliefs, we need to be in it for the long haul.

Simulating the Odds Third-Party Candidates

> "I'm not voting for Genocide Joe! I'm going to vote for a third-party because that's the right thing to do!"

One of the most common conversations when it comes to political division in the USA is whether or not we should or even can vote for a third-party candidate, even though the risk of defeat is high.

Before I get further into this, I want to clarify that genocide, war, terrorism, and the murder of civilians are all unacceptable actions, regardless of who's conducting them. As a result, I fully agree that we need another political party that is in opposition to meaningless and brutal death.

So, what realistically would happen if we started voting for third-party candidates? Mathematically, is it a real possibility? How many third-party voters would it take in each state to win a third-party presidency?

Well, let's look at the math.

For this exercise, I wanted to make a digital simulation of the 2020 election, since at the time of writing that was the most recent presidential election. To do this, I gathered all the available data for the 2020 presidential election. This data includes Electoral College data, as well as Democrat, Republican, and third-party votes by state. I then compiled the total adult population so I could estimate non-voter percentages by state.

After that, I plugged all this data together and created an interactive spreadsheet calculator. You can download this sheet from my website for free. Essentially, this calculator allows you to type in what percentage of voters whom you would like to see vote for a single third-party candidate. You can also decide if those votes should be taken from Democrats, Republicans, or Non-Voters.

After you decide these percentages, the calculator will do the math for you and break it down by state. You'll be able to see which states won which candidates, the new national popular vote, and the new electoral college results.

Again, if you want the calculator, it's free on my website. You can play around with it.

But now that all that is out of the way, let's do some math. One of the most common talking points about the legitimacy of Third-Party candidates is the fact that approximately one-third of the United States population doesn't vote each election cycle.

So, of course, the very first thing I wanted to know is how many non-voters it would take to create a third-party presidency without anyone else switching their vote.

So, for this experiment, let's say we have a new third-party candidate who's taking the country by storm. Let's call her Jane Q. Public.

Let's say, Jane's specifically going after non-voters so every single vote for Joe Biden and Donald Trump remained unchanged, but 100% of registered voters who didn't vote in the 2020 election came together and voted for Ms. Public.

Doing the math, it turns out that even if 100% of non-voters voted for Jane, she still would not have won in any of the states, however, she would've beaten Trump in the popular vote.

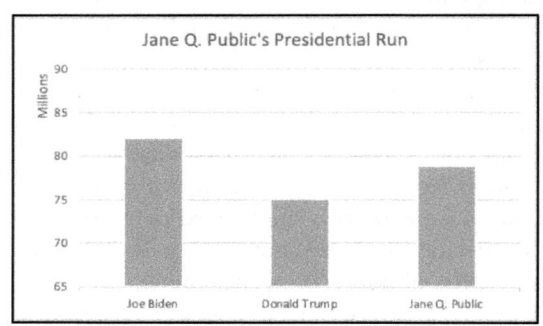

Figure 56: Popular Vote if 100% of Non-Voters Voted for Jane Q. Public

That being said, the presidential election would've had exactly the same results.

This, again, is due to the Electoral College. About a third of the United States did not cast their vote in 2020, and that third was not enough to overtake the 2020 winner in any state.

As a result, even though Ms. Public would've taken one-third of all the votes, she wouldn't have won a single point in the Electoral College.

So... then I decided to look up some realistic statistics.

Let's start with approval ratings. These are taken from Five-Thirty-Eight and at the time of writing, about 54% of Democratic voters disapprove of Joe Biden. (Thomson-DeVeaux, Mithani and Bronner 2020) This is compared to only 19% of Republican voters who don't approve of Donald Trump.

So, without factoring in non-voters, if 54% of Democrats and 19% of Republicans decided to vote for Jane Q. Public, what would happen?

Well, first off, every single blue state would flip to another party. Out of those states, Trump would win Arizona, Georgia, Michigan, Nevada, and Wisconsin. Jane Q Public would win all the others. Trump, on the other hand, would not lose any states.

As a result, the Republicans would win both the popular vote and the Electoral College with 312 electoral points.

Figure 57: Electoral College Map Simulating a 54% Democratic Switch and 19% Republican Switch

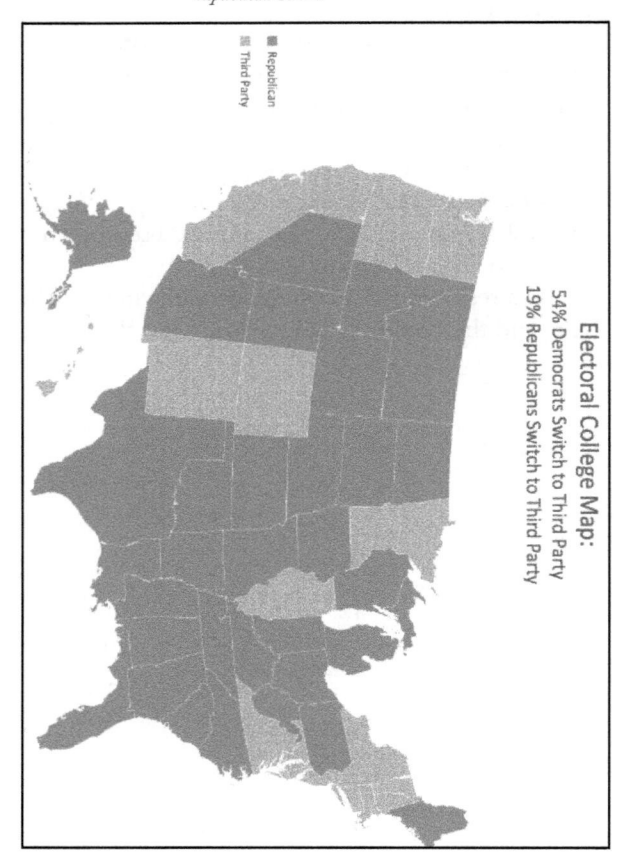

Electoral College Map:
54% Democrats Switch to Third Party
19% Republicans Switch to Third Party

■ Republican
▩ Third Party

So, next, I decided to look up to see how many non-voters would have to vote for Jane to switch this. It comes out to around 8%. Now, according to Five-Thirty-Eight, about 25% of nonvoters said they didn't vote because they didn't like either candidate.

So that means that Jane would need to win the hearts of 54% of the Democratic voters, 19% of the Republican voters, and 32% of the people who refused to vote because they didn't like any candidate.

And again, if there were multiple third-party candidates in the election, the Republicans would still win unless all the third-party voters chose Jane. That's incredibly unlikely.

However, if that were to happen, Ms. Public would make it to 306 electoral college points and win the presidency.

I feel the need to remind you, however, that this scenario is the minimum it would take using the approval ratings from Five-Thirty-Eight. This is the bare minimum requirement for a third-party to win, yet nearly a fifth of all Republicans, over half of all Democrats, and a third of the non-voters who didn't like either one would need to all agree on one single person. Not just that, but that candidate would need to be so fundamentally impressive that Democratic and Republican voters would want to risk the presidency to vote for them.

Figure 58: Electoral College Map Simulating a 54% Democratic Switch, 19% Republican Switch, and 8% Non-Voter Switch to Third-Party

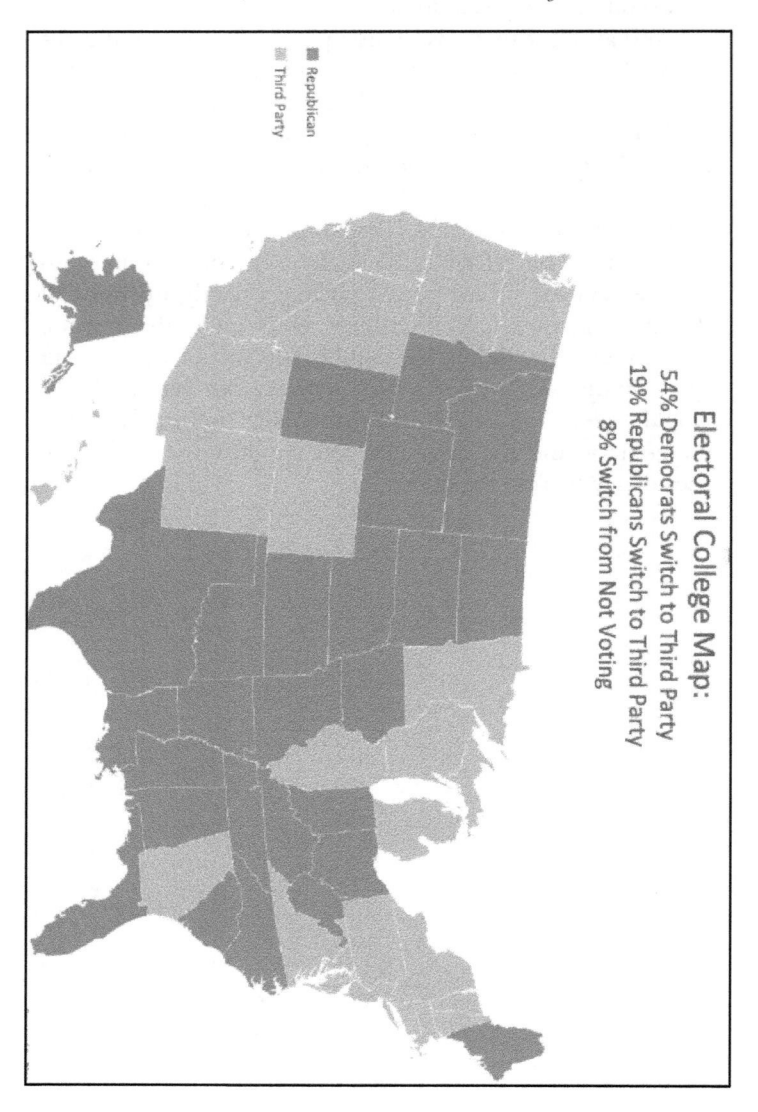

Unfortunately, the fact is, the most likely scenario if we

start voting for Third-Party candidates is that the Republicans will start winning more and more elections. As discussed in the previous chapters, if you're a leftist or liberal, this will give you the opposite of your desired result.

So long story short, if we wanted a third party to be another major party in the United States, to do that safely and reliably, we would need to eliminate the Electoral College and institute rank-choice voting before we start trying.

This isn't my opinion; this isn't a claim based on my feelings or what has happened in history; this is math. The way the Electoral College is designed implicitly stops a third-party candidate from winning the presidency.

There's a reason that Bernie is a Democrat every time he runs for president.

Simulating the Odds of a Third-Party Celebrity

> "No, third parties need MORE ATTENTION! We need a beloved celebrity, like Taylor Swift to run as a Third-Party candidate!"

Okay... I thought this was clear already, but everyone loves Taylor Swift so let's see how well she does.

Just like the other examples, I'm going to base it on the 2020 election results. So we have Biden versus Trump, and then we need to throw Taylor Swift into it. So how are we going to do that?

Well, we have to find how many people would actually vote for Taylor Swift. According to Forbes, about 53% of the US adult population said that they were fans of Taylor

Swift, which is, which is a lot, that's like, that's more than half the population. (Dellatto 2023) But how many would actually vote for Taylor Swift? According to Pew Research, only about 66% of eligible voters voted in the last election. (Igielnik, Keeter and Hartig 2021)

Assuming that every single person who was going to vote anyway voted for Taylor Swift, that would mean about 35% of the eligible voter base would vote for Taylor Swift instead of Trump or Biden.

For this model, we're going to assume that Taylor Swift's votes will be equally pulled from Democratic and Republican voters, which seems unlikely. However, since I couldn't find a legitimate source that goes over the political affiliation of Swifties, the best way to manage affiliation is to treat both parties equally. Plus, if I switched a higher percentage of Democrats to third-party than Republicans, we'd just be repeating our last experiment.

So in this scenario, 35% of the Democratic Votes will be pulled from Joe Biden and 35% will be pulled from Donald Trump.

How does this shake out?

Well... Taylor Swift wins the popular vote, which is good news if you're a Swifty.

In this model, our girl Taylor gets 55 million votes, outpacing the incumbent Joe Biden by nearly 2 million, and coming way ahead of Donald Trump by a little over 6 million votes.

Figure 59: A bar chart of the simulated popular vote result for a 2020 Election in which Taylor Swift ran third-party.

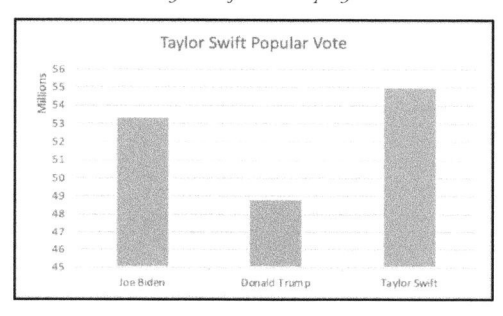

But... things go awry when we start looking at the Electoral College. Taylor Swift wins 177 electoral college votes, while Donald Trump wins 149, and Joe Biden wins 212.

Figure 60: Electoral College Map Simulating a 54% Democratic Switch, 19% Republican Switch, and 8% Non-Voter Switch to Third-Party

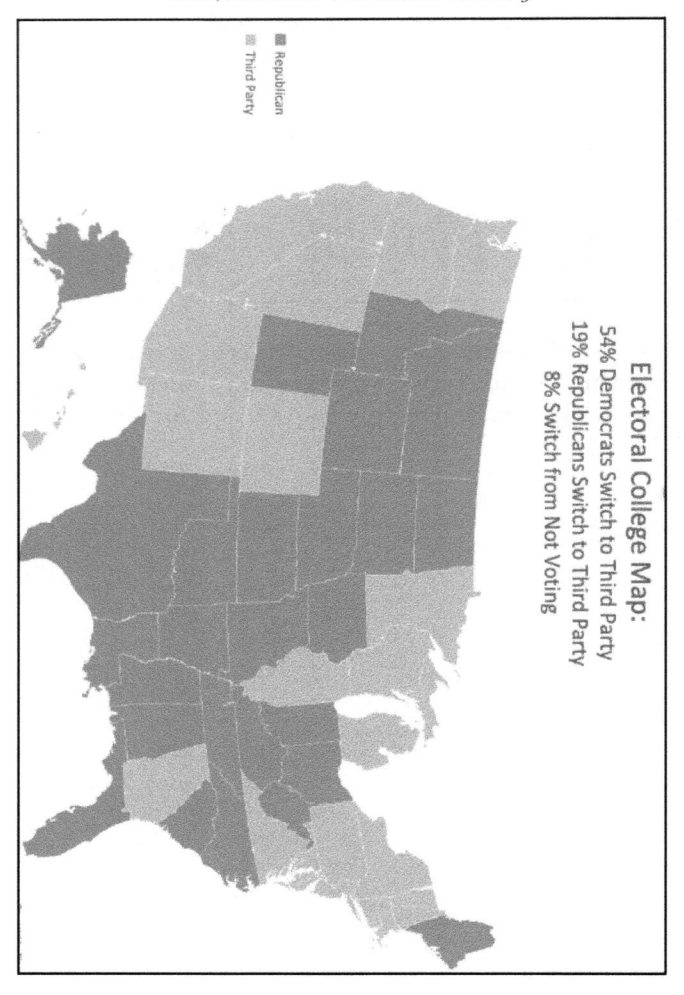

So, even though Taylor takes 13 states away from Biden and Trump, she still doesn't win the election because of the Electoral College.

But here's the thing... Biden doesn't win the election

either. Biden only has 212 Electoral Votes, which isn't enough. Candidates need to win 270 electoral votes to win the presidential election. So, what happens next? We'd have to go into a contingent election, in which case the House of Representatives would decide the President of the United States.

Of course, the House has 435 members, but in a contingent election, the House reps don't vote one at a time. Instead, it goes state by state within the House of Representatives.

Unfortunately, this means in this scenario, if Taylor Swift were to run for the president of the United States as a third party, even though she would likely win the popular vote, and Joe Biden would likely win the electoral vote, the House of Representatives has the highest likelihood of electing Donald Trump as the new president.

So... maybe let's re-think our strategy.

If all of us Voted for a Third-Party Candidate

"If 100% of Democrats voted for a Third Party Candidate, we'd elect a Third-Party. The problem is the lack of people willing to try!"

The number one rebuttal for those who support third parties is the fact that if 100% of Democratic voters switched their vote to Third-Party, the Third-Party candidate would win.

Yes, this is *technically correct* since Democrats won the election in 2020. If we repeated that same election but replaced all Democratic votes with votes for a singular Third-Party candidate, the Third-Party candidate would win, but there are many, many problems with this ideology.

First things first, they would have to agree on a single

candidate, which is unlikely. Can you think of a single candidate from the Green Party, Tea Party, Libertarian Party, etc. that 100% of Democratic voters would agree on? This doesn't just include the leftists, but the liberals and the moderates as well. I sure can't of anyone.

As we referenced several chapters ago, a significant percentage of Biden's voters are moderates.

In fact, approximately 2% more swing voters in 2020 previously voted for Donald Trump in 2016. (Igielnik, Keeter and Hartig 2021) This implies that Biden won over Trump in 2020 at least in part because of the swing voters who lean conservative. Those voters are unlikely to vote for a left-leaning Third-Party candidate.

But that's only 2% of voters, right? Not enough to swing an election.

Here's the thing. If 2% of those who voted for Joe Biden in 2020 switched to a third party, the Republicans would've won.

Here's the breakdown:

Biden would've gotten 269 Electoral College votes and Trump would've also received 269 electoral votes since Arizona, Georgia, and Wisconsin would have flipped from Democratic to Republican.

This would've forced the Presidential race into a congenital election, which allows the House of Representatives to decide based on the state they're from and we've already covered what happens in that scenario.

This means that if just 2% of voters switch their vote, even though Joe Biden would win the popular vote and tie the electoral college vote, he still would likely lose the federal election.

This is the system that we have.

Figure 61: Electoral College Map Simulating a 2% Democratic Switch to Third-Party

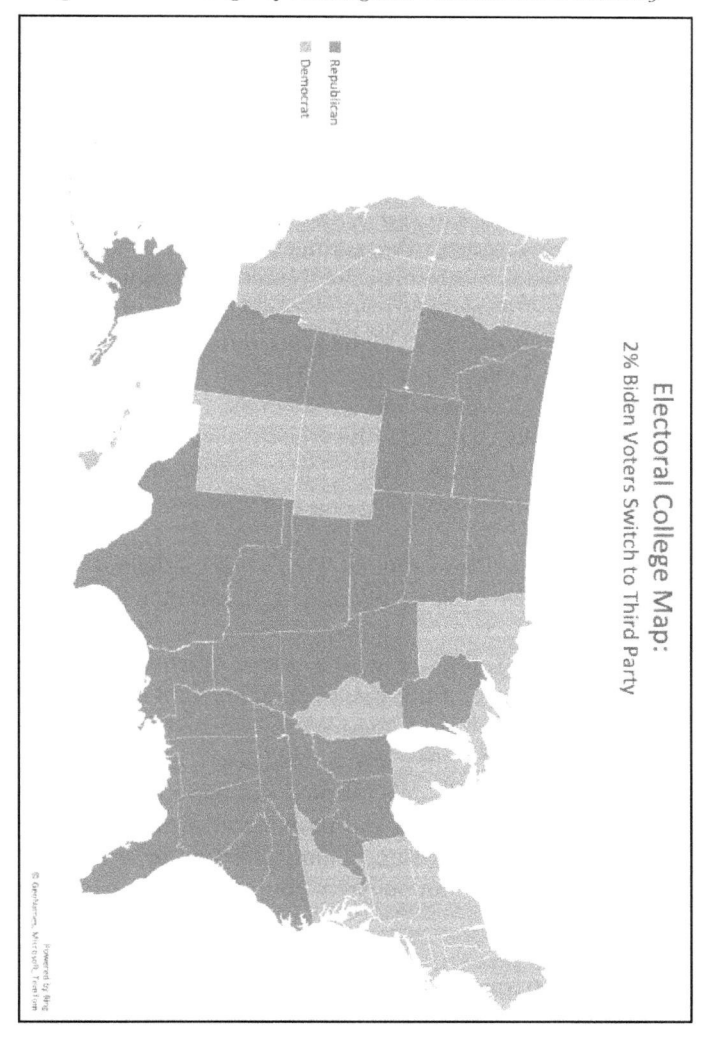

Now, I am not telling you who to vote for.
I am not taking a political stance and I'm not advocating for any particular political candidate. Vote for whoever you

If all of us Voted for a Third-Party Candidate | 133

believe in voting for. I'm just showing you the math.

And if you believe that Joe Biden is a war criminal, if you believe that we shouldn't vote Joe Biden in because of his policies, or even if you just think that he's too old to be the President of the USA, no matter what it is that's stopping you from voting for Joe Biden, ask yourself, "Is he worse than the Republican candidate that he will be facing?"

Keep in mind, I'm not asking if he is worse than the Third-Party candidate. I'm asking if you honestly believe that Joe Biden is worse than the Republican candidate.

If you're a Republican voter considering a third-party candidate, I ask that you do the same thing.

If you do believe that, great. You can vote for a Third Party or the other candidate.

But, thanks to the Electoral College, it's proven statistically that voting Third Party before the Electoral College is eliminated or bypassed is a vote taken from your second choice.

That's not just my opinion. That's not me telling you to vote for. This isn't fearmongering or "bogeyman logic."

That's math.

The math shows that it's very nearly statistically impossible to elect a third-party candidate with the way our elections are set up. And if you're one of those people who really believe that voting for a third party is in your best interest while the electoral college is still there, I urge you to *please* do the math yourself and show us what that looks like. You can go to my website to find the data as well as the calculator. Punch in the numbers yourself and see what you find.

But most importantly, I urge you to take the correct steps to help make it possible for a future third-party candidate.

Voting Third-Party in Protest

"I'm not voting Third-Party so they win, I'm voting Third-Party to start changing the status quo! I understand the chance of a Third-Party candidate winning the presidency is near zero but if Third-Party votes keep increasing, it'll pressure all politicians to do better!"

This again? We've already covered this.

Well, it comes up enough, let's rehash it.

From what I understand, this is the belief that most Third-Party supporters have. If you vote against Democrats long enough, they'll start losing elections and they'll eventually run more left-leaning candidates to earn those votes back. It seems like a fine idea in theory, but in practice it just doesn't work that way. In fact, it works just the opposite.

Here's why—when the Democratic Candidate loses left-leaning voters, they make it up by reaching toward the moderate voters.

Let's take the 2020 election and compare that to 2016. In 2016, the Third-Party vote was primarily split into two camps—Gary Johnson, the Libertarian who received 3.28% of the popular vote, and Jill Stein, the Green Party candidate who received 1.07% of the vote. (Federal Election Commission 2017)

There were other Third-Parties as well. There was an independent candidate, a Constitution Party candidate, and a Socialism and Liberation party candidate.

When you add it all up, the left-leaning Third-Party candidates received 1,531,619 votes. Even though they split the democratic votes, if they hadn't been on the ticket, they likely still wouldn't have been enough to have influenced the election in Clinton's favor. It's theoretically possible, but Clinton would've had to change her entire platform to appease those voters.

The Third-Party candidates who fall into the moderate/conservative category, however, got 5,424,422 votes in total. These were the voters who were more conservative than Clinton, but less conservative than Trump. However, a fraction of those 5 million votes could've easily pushed Hillary Clinton into the presidency, all while those voters were easier to align with than the leftists.

In 2020, Joe Biden went after those moderate/conservative votes and got them. There were only two Third-Party candidates on the ticket—Jo Jorgensen, a Libertarian who got 1.18% of the popular vote, and Howie Hawkins, a Green Party candidate who won .26% of the popular vote. Neither candidate had enough votes to sway the election. In fact, even when you combine the Third-Party votes from 2020 and give them to Donald Trump, they still wouldn't have enough votes to sway the results. (Federal Elections 2020 2022) The large majority of the moderate/conservative swing voters went to Biden, and that's why he won the election.

This process goes back throughout history as well. In the 2020 election, Gore lost 2.74% of the Democratic vote to Nader, the Green Party candidate, yet he still almost won the election.

The DNC learned their lesson in 2008, and they made up the votes with more moderates. Obama approached politics with a more mainstream style. In fact, he later said his policies were so mainstream he'd be seen as a Republican in the 80's. (Swanson 2012) We typically think about Obama as a leftist for his time, but aside from Obamacare, he was very conservative. He opposed gay marriage, but since has flipped his stance. (Bowers 2012) During his administration, he also made many of George W. Bush's tax cuts permanent. (H.R.8 - American Taxpayer Relief Act of 2012 2013)

Because of the conservative push, he was able to win over the moderate voters and overtake McCain and win the election, even while losing leftist votes to Ralph Nader.

Throughout history, when Democrats start losing elections, they get more conservative, not less. They pick up more moderate and conservative votes and win the next election.

As a result, bringing the conversation back to where we began, voting against Biden will not encourage the Democratic National Committee to bring in more left-leaning candidates. In fact, their response throughout modern history is to become more conservative. For better or worse, that strategy has worked for them nearly every time.

Eliminating the Electoral College

"We can't get rid of the Electoral College!"

Contrary to widely held belief, there actually is a way to bypass the Electoral College, and it's surprisingly easy. Not only that, but we could do it right now and states are already working on it. It's called the National Popular Vote Interstate Compact, and essentially, it's an agreement between states. (National Popular Vote n.d.) This agreement ensures that the states who participate in it will award their electoral college votes to the candidate gets the popular vote in the United States federal election, even if the state's popular vote is in the favor of another candidate.

This compact has already been adopted by about 17 states, taking up 205 electoral votes, which equates to 75.9% of what's needed to overtake the electoral college.

It's unlikely that it'll be passed in red states because Republicans typically don't make the popular vote—both George W. Bush and Donald Trump lost the popular vote but became president because of the Electoral College. However, we don't need red states to sign on. If more states joined in and totaled 64 electoral college votes or more, the states in this compact would equal or exceed the 270 votes required to elect a president.

Since we only need 64 additional electoral college votes, we only need the help of Minnesota, Pennsylvania, New Hampshire, Virginia, and Arizona. If those states sign legislation to join the pact, the electoral college would effectively be bypassed, and popular vote would be the deciding factor of who becomes the president of the United States.

With my election calculator, you can actually go through and add states to that compact to see what effect it would have on the election. You can do this with rank choice voting turned on or off, and if it's turned on, you can select the percentage of people that switch to the other party or switch to third party if their party loses anyway.

As a result, this whole idea that we are not moving toward more fair election processes and third parties will just never be able to exist in the United States is very silly. If you believe that Democrats are not working for change or believe that we will never be able to have third parties in the United States, you're not paying attention. But that does not mean that you should vote third party right now, as mentioned in previous chapters.

Third parties aren't viable at this moment; however, with a little work, they might be before the 2028 election.

What Can We Do?

"What now, then?"

That's what it comes down to, right? How can we, the people who live in this country, help fix it?

Well, as you may have guessed, the first thing I'm going to say is "Vote."

Vote.

Vote!

Vote, vote!

Vote in the primaries. Vote in the general election. Vote in local elections. All positions, from your city council to your commissioner, to your mayor, to your governor, to your state House and Senate, to your attorney general, EVERYONE.

Go to your favorite search engine and type "List of elections in" and type your state. Then do the same thing for your city. Make a checklist. Vote in every single one of those.

This cannot be overstated. Vote. Vote often.

But outside of voting, what can you do?

Well, you can also run for office. There is a website called RunForSomething.net that supports new progressive activists. It doesn't matter what your qualifications are, there's something there for you.

If you hate our political climate and don't agree with your current representatives, you have two options: vote against them or run against them.

If you don't want to run, you can volunteer. Local campaigns are expensive and difficult. Volunteer to help. Just call a person running for city council who you agree with and ask what you can do to help them. There will be something. Of course, you can also join protests, sign petitions, help with local nonprofit activist groups, etc.

But what else?

Lastly, you can learn. Learn about how the system works. Study up on the effects of policies or court decisions. Keep learning about whatever you find yourself curious about.

But here's the most important thing—Don't stop. Don't lose focus. Don't give up.

This is how we got to this point. As a society, we have the attention span of a goldfish. When something happens and it captures our attention, we lose focus the second something else happens.

I know it can be overwhelming. Terrible things happen all the time. You can't keep track of all of them.

But it's important to keep putting pressure on the people responsible. Don't let that momentum down.

If a politician continues to vote for legislation that you

disagree with, remember their name. Call that representative, email them. Vote against them. Run against them. Volunteer to help the campaign of the person running against them.

If it doesn't change overnight, don't be surprised. *Of course, it won't!* It's much easier to knock a cup over than to clean up a spill.

Do this until they're out of office, and don't stop a second before.

Don't ever give up.
Keep the pressure on.
Keep going.
All right, the book's over. Go vote.

Table of Figures

Figure 1: Slave Percentages in 1860 as a comparison to Prison Population per 100k in 2024. 9
Figure 2: List of States Grouped by Affiliation ... 18
Figure 3: Violent Crime, Homicide, and School Shooting Averages by Affiliation Groups 21
Figure 4: Wage and Tax Burden by Affiliation Group 24
Figure 5: Average Rent by Affiliation Group 26
Figure 6: Average Monthly Groceries Cost by Affiliation Group 30
Figure 7: Electricity Monthly Cost by Affiliation Group 32
Figure 8: Percentage of Income Removed by Taxes, Rent, Food, and Power 33
Figure 9: Job Hires, Layoffs, and Firings by Affiliation Group 37
Figure 10: Homicide and Income Remaining after Expenses 40
Figure 11: Violent Crime, Homicide, and School

Shootings by Groups Based on Income Minus Taxes, Rent, Food and Power 42

Figure 12: Most Populous Red Cities in Texas (2019) 45

Figure 13: Violent Crime, Murder Rate, and Rape Rate of Cities in Texas by Political Affiliation in 2019 46

Figure 14: Aggravated Assault, Burglary, and Property Crime Rate of Cities in Texas by Political Affiliation in 2019 47

Figure 15: Most Populous Red Cities in Illinois .. 48

Figure 16: Violent Crime, Murder Rate, and Rape Rate of Cities in Illinois by Political Affiliation in 2019 49

Figure 17: Violent Crime, Murder Rate, and Rape Rate of Cities in Illinois with Higher than 25 thousand People by Political Affiliation in 2019 50

Figure 18: Maternal Mortality by Affiliation Group 56

Figure 19: Food Insecure Children by Affiliation Group 58

Figure 20: SAT ERW and Math Scores by Affiliation Group 59

Figure 21: Political Funding from Gun Rights Activist Groups in 2020 62

Figure 22: Political Funding from Gun Rights Activist Groups by Party in 2020 63

Figure 23: Political Funding from For-Profit Prisons in 2020 64

Figure 24: Political Funding from For-Profit Prisons by Party in 2020 64

Figure 25: Political Funding from the Oil and Gas Industry in 2020 65

Figure 26: Political Funding from the Oil and Gas

Industry by Party in 2020 66
    Figure 27: Political Funding from the Oil and Gas Industry by Political Groups in 2020 66
    Figure 28: AIPAC Funding by Party in 2020 67
    Figure 29: Percentage of Candidates Receiving AIPAC Funding by Party in 2020 68
    Figure 30: Political Funding from Universities by Party in 2020 69
    Figure 31: Political Funding from by Party in 2020 70
    Figure 32: Political Funding from Securities and Investments Industry by Party in 2020 71
    Figure 33 Political Funding from Securities and Investments Industry by Political Groups in 2020 72
    Figure 34: Voting in Favor of Unlocking our Domestic LNG Potential Act by Party 77
    Figure 35: Figure 36: Voting in Favor of Consumer Fuel Price Gouging Prevention Act by Party .. 78
    Figure 37: Votes in Favor of the For the People Act 81
    Figure 38: Votes Against the For the People Act 82
    Figure 39: Senate Votes in Favor of the Infrastructure Investment and Jobs Act 83
    Figure 40: Senate Republican Votes in Favor and Against the Infrastructure Investment and Jobs Act 84
    Figure 41: Votes in Favor of the Israel Security Supplemental Appropriations Act 86
    Figure 42: Votes Against the Israel Security Supplemental Appropriations Act 86
    Figure 43: Votes in Favor of the Protecting Americans from Foreign Adversary Controlled Applications Act 88

Figure 44: Votes in Favor of the Protecting Americans from Foreign Adversary Controlled Applications Act 88

Figure 45: Protecting Americans from Foreign Adversary Controlled Applications Act Republican Votes 89

Figure 46: Protecting Americans from Foreign Adversary Controlled Applications Act Democrat Votes 89

Figure 47: A Grid of Electoral Squares 98

Figure 48: Election Grid Divided by Districts 99

Figure 49: Election Grid Divided by 6 Districts 100

Figure 50: Election Grid Divided by 6 Districts - Adjusted Vote in District 2 101

Figure 51: Election Grid Divided by 6 Districts with Added Third-Party 103

Figure 52: Election Grid Divided by 6 Districts - Adjusted Vote in District 2 104

Figure 53: Electoral College Map Simulating a 30% Democratic Switch to Third-Party 108

Figure 54: Electoral College Map Simulating a 30% Democratic Switch and 20% Republican Switch to Third-Party 109

Figure 55: Electoral College Map Simulating a 35% Democratic Switch, 30% Republican Switch, and 5% Non-Voter Switch to Third-Party 111

Figure 56: Popular Vote if 100% of Non-Voters Voted for Jane Q. Public 118

Figure 57: Electoral College Map Simulating a 54% Democratic Switch and 19% Republican Switch 120

Figure 58: Electoral College Map Simulating a 54% Democratic Switch, 19% Republican Switch, and 8%

Non-Voter Switch to Third-Party 122

Figure 59: A bar chart of the simulated popular vote result for a 2020 Election in which Taylor Swift ran third-party..127

Figure 60: Electoral College Map Simulating a 54% Democratic Switch, 19% Republican Switch, and 8% Non-Voter Switch to Third-Party 128

Figure 61: Electoral College Map Simulating a 2% Democratic Switch to Third-Party 133

Bibliography

1864. "1860 Census: Population of the United States." *United States Census.* https://www.census.gov/library/publications/1864/dec/1860a.html.

n.d. *2023 Rent Data by State.* https://www.rentdata.org/states/2023.

1962. "A Century of Lawmaking for a New Nation: U.S. Congressional Documents and Debates, 1774 - 1875." *The Library of Congress.* A Century of Lawmaking for a New Nation: U.S. Congressional Documents and Debates, 1774 - 1875.

2023. *A Guide to U.S. Retail Pricing Laws and Regulations.* May 11. https://www.nist.gov/pml/owm/laws-and-regulations/us-retail-pricing-laws-and-regulations.

n.d. *About.* https://energycommerce.house.gov/about.

n.d. *About the Governor.* https://governor.vermont.gov/about-us.

2024. *American Israel Public Affairs Cmte.* March 6. https://www.opensecrets.org/orgs/american-israel-public-affairs-cmte/recipients?toprecipscycle=2024&id=D000046963&candscycle=2020.

Ashbrook, Alexandra. 2022. *Food Research & Action Center.* November 11. https://frac.org/blog/too-many-veterans-battle-with-hunger.

Berkowitz, Seth A, Sanjay Basu, Craig Gunderson, and Hilary Seligman. 2019. "State-Level and County-Level Estimates of Health Care Costs Associated with Food Insecurity." *National Center for Chronic Disease Prevention and Health Promotion.* https://doi.org/10.5888/pcd16.180549.

n.d. *Bernie Sanders.* https://www.biography.com/political-figures/bernie-sanders.

Bowers, Becky. 2012. *President Barack Obama's shifting stance on gay marriage.* May 11. https://www.politifact.com/factchecks/2012/may/11/barack-obama/president-barack-obamas-shift-gay-marriage/.

Cheng, Allen. n.d. *Average SAT Scores by State.* https://blog.prepscholar.com/average-sat-scores-by-state-most-recent.

2016. *Classification 50: Involuntary Servitude and Slavery.*

August 15. https://www.archives.gov/research/investigations/fbi/classifications/050-slavery.html.

n.d. *Crime Data Explorer*. https://cde.ucr.cjis.gov/LATEST/webapp/#/pages/downloads.

Current, Richard N. 2024. *Abraham Lincoln*. March 14. https://www.britannica.com/biography/Abraham-Lincoln.

Dam, Andrew Van. 2023. "The real reason red states are hiring so much faster than blue states." *The Washington Post*, May 26. https://www.washingtonpost.com/business/2023/05/26/hiring-red-blue-states/.

n.d. *Definitions of Food Security*. https://www.ers.usda.gov/topics/food-nutrition-assistance/food-security-in-the-u-s/definitions-of-food-security/.

Dellatto, Marisa. 2023. "More Than Half Of U.S. Adults Say They're Taylor Swift Fans, Survey Finds." *Forbes*, March 14. https://www.forbes.com/sites/marisadellatto/2023/03/14/more-than-half-of-us-adults-say-theyre-taylor-swift-fans-survey-finds/.

Desjardins, Lisa, and Dorothy Hastings. 2022. *Democrats unveil new plan to increase taxes on billionaires*. March 30. https://www.pbs.org/newshour/show/democrat

s-unveil-new-plan-to-increase-taxes-on-billionaires.

2024. "Detailed Data Tool." *The Sentencing Project*. March 18.
https://www.sentencingproject.org/app/uploads/2024/03/TSP-State-Data-2024-3-18.xlsx.

n.d. *Directory of Representatives*.
https://www.house.gov/representatives.

n.d. *Distribution of Electoral Votes*.
https://www.archives.gov/electoral-college/allocation.

2021. *Education Summary*. March 22.
https://www.opensecrets.org/industries/indus?cycle=2020&ind=W04.

n.d. *Electricity Data Browser*.
https://www.eia.gov/electricity/data/browser/.

n.d. *Every Town Research*. Accessed 2023.
https://everytownresearch.org/report/fact-sheet-preemption-laws.

n.d. *Explore Tables*. https://data.census.gov/table.

Fall, James A. 2019. *Alaska Population Trends and Patterns 1960-2018*. The Alaska Department of Fish and Game.
https://www.adfg.alaska.gov/static/home/library/pdfs/subsistence/Trends_in_Population_Summary_2019.pdf.

Federal Election Commission. 2017. *Federal Elections 2016*. Federal Election Commission. https://www.fec.gov/resources/cms-content/documents/federalelections2016.pdf.

———. 2022. *Federal Elections 2020*. Federal Election Commission. https://www.fec.gov/resources/cms-content/documents/federalelections2020.pdf.

———. 2021. *For Profit Prisons*. March 22. https://www.opensecrets.org/industries/recips?cycle=2020&ind=G7000.

Garrett-Scott, Shennette, Rebecca Cummings Richardson, and Venita Dillard-Allen. 2013. ""When Peace Come": Teaching the Significance of Juneteenth." *Association for the Study of African American Life and History* 76 (2): 19-25.

Glass, Andrew. 2019. *Politico*. February 25. https://www.politico.com/story/2019/02/25/this-day-in-politics-february-25-1180225.

———. n.d. *Governors*. https://www.nga.org/governors/.

———. 2021. *Gun Rights Summary*. March 22. https://www.opensecrets.org/industries/indus?cycle=2020&ind=Q13.

———. 2021. *H.R.1 - For the People Act of 2021*. January 4. https://www.congress.gov/bill/117th-congress/house-bill/1?loclr=bloglaw.

———. 2021. *H.R.1319 - American Rescue Plan Act of 2021*. March 11. https://www.congress.gov/bill/117th-congress/house-bill/1319/text.

2024. *H.R.7176 - Unlocking our Domestic LNG Potential Act of 2024*. February 15.
https://energycommerce.house.gov/about.

2024. *H.R.7217 - Israel Security Supplemental Appropriations Act, 2024*. February 5.
https://www.congress.gov/bill/118th-congress/house-bill/7217/text.

2022. *H.R.7688 - Consumer Fuel Price Gouging Prevention Act*. May 6. https://www.congress.gov/bill/117th-congress/house-bill/7688.

2013. *H.R.8 - American Taxpayer Relief Act of 2012*. January 2. https://www.congress.gov/bill/112th-congress/house-bill/8.

Hartig, Hanna, Andrew Daniller, Scott Keeter, and Ted Van Green. 2023. *Republican Gains in 2022 Midterms Driven Mostly by Turnout Advantage*. Pew Research Center, 2.
https://www.pewresearch.org/politics/2023/07/12/voting-patterns-in-the-2022-elections/.

Heimbach, Alex. n.d. *Which States Require the SAT? Complete List*. https://blog.prepscholar.com/average-sat-scores-by-state-most-recent.

n.d. *History of Federal Minimum Wage Rates Under the Fair Labor Standards Act, 1938 - 2009*.
https://www.dol.gov/agencies/whd/minimum-wage/history/chart.

History.com Editors. 2021. *Republican Party.* February 1. https://www.history.com/topics/us-government-and-politics/republican-party.

—. 2009. *Ronald Reagan.* November 9. https://www.history.com/topics/us-presidents/ronald-reagan.

1862. *Homestead Act.* May 20. https://www.archives.gov/milestone-documents/homestead-act.

2022. *Homicide Mortality by State.* March 2. https://www.cdc.gov/nchs/pressroom/sosmap/homicide_mortality/homicide.htm.

Igielnik, Ruth, Scott Keeter, and Hannah Hartig. 2021. *Behind Biden's 2020 Victory.* Pew Research Center. https://www.pewresearch.org/politics/2021/06/30/behind-bidens-2020-victory/.

n.d. *Industry Breakdown.* https://www.opensecrets.org/political-action-committees-pacs/industry-breakdown/2020.

Kaufman, Phillip R., James M MacDonald, Steve M. Lutz, and David M Smallwood. 1997. *Do the Poor Pay More for Food? Item Selection and Price Differences Affect Low-Income Household Food Costs.* Agricultural Economic Report, Food and Rural Economics Division, Washington, DC: U.S. Department of Agriculture. https://www.ers.usda.gov/webdocs/publications/40816/32372_aer759.pdf.

Kintzle, Sara. 2018. "PTSD in U.S. Veterans: The Role of Social Connectedness, Combat Experience and Discharge." *Healthcare.*

Lewis, Nicole, Aviva Shen, and Anna Flagg. 2020. *What Do We Really Know About the Politics of People Behind Bars?* March 11. https://www.themarshallproject.org/2020/03/11/what-do-we-really-know-about-the-politics-of-people-behind-bars.

n.d. *Lincoln and the Founding of the National Banking System.* https://www.occ.gov/about/who-we-are/history/founding-occ-national-bank-system/lincoln-and-the-founding-of-the-national-banking-system.html.

Liptak, Kevin. 2022. "Biden's political and personal evolution on abortion on display after publication of draft Supreme Court opinion." *CNN*, May 3. https://www.cnn.com/2022/05/03/politics/joe-biden-abortion-draft-opinion/index.html.

Macilwain, Colin. 1998. "Gore calls for action on climate change as Congress stalls." *Nature*, July 23. https://www.nature.com/articles/28447.

Marotta, David John. 2013. "Dwight D. Eisenhower on tax cuts and a balanced budget." *Forbes*, February 28. https://www.forbes.com/sites/davidmarotta/2013/02/28/dwight-d-eisenhower-on-tax-cuts-and-a-balanced-budget/?sh=4c56b5505047.

Maruschak, Laura M., Jennifer Bronson, and Mariel Alper. 2021. *Veterans in Prison: Survey of Prison Inmates, 2016.* Publication, Bureau of Justice Statistics, Bureau of Justice Statistics. https://bjs.ojp.gov/library/publications/veterans-prison-survey-prison-inmates-2016.

n.d. "Maternal deaths and mortality rates: Each state, the District of Columbia, United States, 2018-2021." *Centers for Disease Control and Prevention.* https://www.cdc.gov/nchs/maternal-mortality/MMR-2018-2021-State-Data.pdf.

n.d. *Members.* https://budget.house.gov/about/members.

Morgan, Dominique, interview by Darius Rafieyan and Cardiff Garcia. 2020. *The Uncounted Workforce* (June 29).

Morris, Kathy. 2022. *The states with the most (and least) people on food stamps.* August 29. https://www.zippia.com/advice/10-states-people-food-stamps/.

National Homelessness Law Center. 2021. *First National Study of State Laws Criminalizing Homelessness Released.* Washington D.C.: National Homelessness Law Center. https://homelesslaw.org/first-national-study-of-state-laws-criminalizing-homelessness-released/.

n.d. *National Popular Vote.* H.R.8 - American Taxpayer Relief Act of 2012.

National Republican Convention. 1860. "National Republican Platform." *Libary of Congress*. May 17. https://www.loc.gov/resource/rbpe.0180010b/?st=text.

Neilsberg Research. 2023. *United States Population by Age*. September 17. https://www.neilsberg.com/insights/united-states-population-by-age/.

Neuman, Scott. 2022. "Adnan Syed's case is unique. Withholding of potentially exculpatory evidence is not." *National Public Radio*, September 21.

Newport, Frank, and Sangeeta Agrawal. 2011. "Democrats Lead Ranks of Both Union and State Workers." *Gallup*, March 24.

Nisbet, Jack, and Claire Nisbet. 2011. "President Abraham Lincoln signs the Revenue Act, which includes the first federal income tax, on August 5, 1861." *HistoryLink.org*. September 14. https://www.historylink.org/File/9914.

2021. *Oil & Gas Summary*. March 22. https://www.opensecrets.org/industries/indus?cycle=2020&ind=E01.

Oxner, Reese. 2021. "Statewide ban on homeless encampments approved by Texas Senate." *The Texas Tribune*, May 20.

Pariona, Amber. 2018. *WorldAtlas*. September 28.

2020. "Party Platform." *The Democratic National Committee*.

July 27. file:///C:/Users/nicho/Downloads/2020-Democratic-Party-Platform%20(1).pdf.

Peck, Emily. 2023. "The median age in the U.S. reaches a record high, approaching 40 years old." *Axios*, June 22.

n.d. *Percent change in average weekly wages by state, total covered employment.* Accessed 2024. https://www.bls.gov/charts/county-employment-and-wages/percent-change-aww-by-state.htm.

2023. *Prevalence of food insecurity, average 2020-22.* October 25. https://www.ers.usda.gov/topics/food-nutrition-assistance/food-security-in-the-u-s/key-statistics-graphics/.

Richter, Paul, and Ronald Brownstein. 1999. "Gore Calls for Compassion in Military's 'Don't Ask, Don't Tell' Policy on Gays : Politics: Vice president says that he does not believe the rules are working properly. Issue remains controversial among presidential rivals." *Los Angeles Times*, August 31. https://www.latimes.com/archives/la-xpm-1999-aug-31-mn-5352-story.html.

Rimkus, Ron. 2013. *President Nixon: The Man Who Sold the World Fiat Money.* March 13. https://blogs.cfainstitute.org/investor/2013/03/13/president-nixon-the-man-who-sold-the-world-fiat-money/.

Roberts, Joe. 2023. *The Average Cost of Food in the US.*

October 24. https://www.move.org/the-average-cost-of-food-in-the-us/.

2019. *Roll Call 496 | Bill Number: H. R. 582.* July 18. Dwight D. Eisenhower on tax cuts and a balanced budget.

2021. *Roll Call Vote 117th Congress - 1st Session.* March 6. https://www.senate.gov/legislative/LIS/roll_call_votes/vote1171/vote_117_1_00110.htm#position.

2021. *Roll Call Vote 117th Congress - 1st Session.* August 10. https://www.senate.gov/legislative/LIS/roll_call_votes/vote1171/vote_117_1_00314.htm.

Rothman, Lily. 2018. *Time.* December 1. https://time.com/3649511/george-hw-bush-quote-read-my-lips.

Save On Energy Team. 2023. *Electricity Bill Report.* https://www.saveonenergy.com/resources/electricity-bills-by-state/.

2021. *Securities & Investment Summary.* March 22. https://www.opensecrets.org/industries/indus?cycle=2020&ind=F07.

Seelye, Katharine Q., and Steven Greenhouse. 1999. "Gore Gains Labor Backing, Minus 2 Powerful Unions." *The New York Times*, October 14. https://www.nytimes.com/1999/10/14/us/gore-gains-labor-backing-minus-2-powerful-unions.html.

n.d. *Senators*. https://www.senate.gov/senators.

n.d. *Shooting Incidents at K-12 Schools (Jan 1970-Jun 2022)*. Accessed 2023. www.chds.us/sssc/data-map/.

Shrikant, Aditi. 2023. "Youth suicide rates rose 62% from 2007 to 2021: 'People feel hopeless,' one recent grad says." *CNBC*, December 5. https://www.cnbc.com/2023/12/05/youth-suicide-rates-rose-62percent-from-2007-to-2021.htm.

n.d. *St. George's Institute*. https://stgeorgesinstitute.org/mycore/courses/his-301/lessons/movements-towards-emancipation/topic/arguments-for-and-against-slavery/.

2022. *State and Local Tax Burdens, Calendar Year 2022*. April 7. https://taxfoundation.org/data/all/state/tax-burden-by-state-2022/.

2023. *Suicide Rates by State*. May 1. Accessed 2024. https://www.cdc.gov/suicide/suicide-rates-by-state.html.

Swanson, Ian. 2012. "Obama says he'd be seen as moderate Republican in 1980s." *The Hill*, December 14. https://thehill.com/policy/finance/137156-obama-says-hed-be-seen-as-moderate-republican-in-1980s/.

n.d. *Table of Supreme Court Justices*.

https://constitution.congress.gov/resources/supreme-court-justices/?loclr=bloglaw.

Tarter, Brent. 2020. *Vagrancy Act of 1866*. December 7.

2022. *Teen Birth Rate by State*. February 25. https://www.cdc.gov/nchs/pressroom/sosmap/teen-births/teenbirths.htm.

Terrell, Ellen. 2021. *The Convict Leasing System: Slavery in its Worst Aspects*. jUN 17. https://blogs.loc.gov/inside_adams/2021/06/convict-leasing-system.

The Associated Press. 2004. "Kerry affirms strong support of abortion rights." *NBC News*, April 23. https://www.nbcnews.com/id/wbna4815646.

—. 2004. "Kerry's positions on gay marriage." *NBC News*, February 11. https://www.nbcnews.com/id/wbna4245324.

The Editors of Encyclopaedia Britannica. 2024. *Bull Moose Party*. February 9. https://www.britannica.com/topic/Bull-Moose-Party.

2023. *The White House*. June 14. https://www.whitehouse.gov/briefing-room/legislation/2023/06/14/bill-signed-s-777.

Thomson-DeVeaux, Amelia, Jasmine Mithani, and Laura Bronner. 2020. "Why Many Americans Don't Vote." *FiveThirtyEight*, October 26. https://projects.fivethirtyeight.com/non-voters-poll-2020-election/.

2023. *Total Deaths due to Firearms by Race/Ethnicity.* April 5. https://www.kff.org/other/state-indicator/firearms-death-rate-by-raceethnicity/.

Trump, Donald. 2017. *The White House.* December 2022. https://trumpwhitehouse.archives.gov/briefings-statements/remarks-president-trump-signing-h-r-1-tax-cuts-jobs-bill-act-h-r-1370.

n.d. *Tufts University Prison Divestment.* https://sites.tufts.edu/prisondivestment/prison-labor/.

U.S. Department of the Interior Bureau of Land Management. 2016. "The Federal Land Policy and Management Act of 1976." *Bureau of Land Management.* September. https://www.blm.gov/sites/default/files/AboutUs_LawsandRegs_FLPMA.pdf.

2023. *United States Congress.* January 25. https://www.congress.gov/bill/118th-congress/house-bill/23.

1865. "United States National Archives." *13th Amendment to the U.S. Constitution: Abolition of Slavery.* January 31. https://www.archives.gov/milestone-documents/13th-amendment.

2020. *Vermont Election Results.* November. https://www.cnn.com/election/2020/results/state/vermont.

Vestal, Allan James, Andrew Briz, Annette Choi, Beatrice Jin, Andrew McGill, and Lily Mihalik. 2021. *Presidential election results*. https://www.politico.com/2020-election/results/president/.

Volpe, Richard, Edward Roeger, and Ephraim Leibtag. 2013. *How Transportation Costs Affect Fresh Fruit and Vegetable Prices*. Economic Research Service.

Williams, Bob. 2017. *Don't Leave Rural California Behind*. August 21. https://cafwd.org/news/dont-leave-rural-california-behind/.

2024. *Workers' rights preemption in the U.S.* February. https://www.epi.org/preemption-map/.

Index

Alabama, 9, 11, 20, 110, 119, 121, 127, 131
Alaska, 9, 19, 27, 80, 110, 119, 121, 127, 131
Arizona, 9, 19, 106, 110, 118, 119, 121, 127, 130, 131, 138
Arkansas, 9, 11, 20, 110, 119, 121, 127, 131
Biden, Joe, 15, 52, 82, 96, 106, 108, 109, 114, 117, 124,
    125, 126, 127, 128, 130, 132, 134, 135
Bush, George W., 14, 96, 112, 135, 138
California, 9, 19, 27, 69, 84, 110, 119, 121, 127, 131
Clinton, Bill, 113
Clinton, Hillary, 96, 113, 114, 134
Colorado, 9, 19, 106, 110, 119, 121, 127, 131
Connecticut, 9, 18, 31, 110, 119, 121, 127, 131
Crime
    Homicide, 21, 41, 42
    Rape, 22, 46, 49, 50
    School Shootings, 42
    Violent Crime, 20, 21, 39, 42, 44, 46, 49
Delaware, 9, 18, 110, 119, 121, 127, 131
Democratic Party, 6, 7, 15, 16, 18, 19, 35, 36, 38, 51, 52,
    61, 63, 68, 71, 76, 77, 79, 80, 81, 83, 88, 89, 90, 94, 95,
    96, 106, 108, 111, 116, 117, 119, 120, 122, 125, 129, 130,

133, 135
Education, 2, 53, 55, 57, 58, 60, 79, 102
Eisenhower, Dwight D., 14
Employment
    Job Hires, 37
    Layoffs, 36, 38
    Quits, 38
    Wages, 12, 22, 23, 35, 38, 159
Federal Bureau of Investigation (FBI), 20, 44, 47
Fiat Currency, 8
Florida, 9, 19, 40, 101, 107, 108, 110, 119, 121, 127, 131
Ford, Gerald, 13, 14
Georgia, 9, 11, 19, 40, 106, 107, 108, 110, 118, 119, 121, 127, 130, 131
Gore, Al, 112, 113, 135
Green Party, 130, 134, 135
Gun Rights Activist Groups, 62, 63, 67, 73
H.R. 1 - For the People Act of 2021, 80
H.R. 1319 - Rescue Plan Act of 2021, 78
H.R. 3684 - the Infrastructure Investment and Jobs Act, 82
H.R. 582, or the Raise the Wage Act, 15
H.R. 7176, the Unlocking our Domestic LNG Potential Act of 2024, 76
H.R. 7217 - the Israel Security Supplemental Appropriations Act of 2024, 84
H.R. 7688 - Consumer Fuel Price Gouging Prevention Act, 77
Hawaii, 9, 18, 40, 107, 108, 110, 119, 121, 127, 131
Homestead Act of 1862, 11, 13
Idaho, 9, 20, 40, 107, 108, 110, 119, 121, 127, 131
Illinois, 9, 19, 40, 48, 49, 50, 106, 107, 108, 110, 119, 121, 127, 131
Immigration, 12, 75
Indiana, 9, 19, 40, 107, 108, 110, 119, 121, 127, 131
Internal Revenue Service (IRS), 7
Iowa, 9, 20, 40, 107, 108, 110, 119, 121, 127, 131
Juneteenth, 10

Kansas, 9, 19, 40, 107, 108, 110, 119, 121, 127, 131
Kentucky, 9, 19, 40, 107, 108, 110, 119, 121, 127, 131
Kerry, John, 113
Legal Tender Act of 1862, 8
Libertarian Ideology, 8
Libertarian Party, 130
Lincoln, Abraham, 6, 7, 8, 11, 12, 13, 14, 15, 16
Louisiana, 9, 11, 19, 40, 107, 108, 110, 119, 121, 127, 131
Maine, 9, 19, 40, 44, 105, 106, 107, 108, 110, 119, 121, 127, 131
Maryland, 9, 19, 31, 40, 80, 107, 108, 110, 119, 121, 127, 131
Massachusetts, 9, 18, 31, 40, 107, 108, 110, 119, 121, 127, 131
McCain, John, 135
Michigan, 9, 19, 40, 106, 107, 108, 110, 118, 119, 121, 127, 131
Minimum Wage, 14
Minnesota, 9, 19, 40, 106, 107, 108, 110, 119, 121, 127, 131, 138
Mississippi, 9, 11, 19, 40, 107, 108, 110, 119, 121, 127, 131
Missouri, 9, 19, 40, 107, 108, 110, 119, 121, 127, 131
Montana, 9, 19, 40, 107, 108, 110, 119, 121, 127, 131
National Banking Acts of 1863 and 1864, 13
Nebraska, 9, 20, 40, 105, 106, 107, 108, 110, 119, 121, 127, 131
Nevada, 9, 19, 40, 107, 108, 110, 118, 119, 121, 127, 131
New Hampshire, 9, 19, 31, 40, 44, 106, 107, 108, 110, 119, 121, 127, 131, 138
New Jersey, 9, 19, 31, 40, 106, 107, 108, 110, 119, 121, 127, 131
New Mexico, 9, 18, 40, 106, 107, 108, 110, 119, 121, 127, 131
New York, 9, 19, 31, 40, 107, 108, 110, 119, 121, 127, 131
Nixon, Richard, 14
North Carolina, 9, 19, 40, 107, 108, 110, 119, 121, 127, 131
North Dakota, 9, 20, 40, 107, 108, 110, 119, 121, 127, 131

Obama, Barack, 113, 135
Ocasio-Cortez, Alexandria, 96
Ohio, 9, 19, 40, 107, 108, 110, 119, 121, 127, 131
Oklahoma, 9, 20, 40, 107, 108, 110, 119, 121, 127, 131
Oregon, 9, 19, 31, 40, 106, 107, 108, 110, 119, 121, 127, 131
Pacific Railway Act, 14
Pennsylvania, 9, 19, 40, 106, 107, 108, 110, 119, 121, 127, 131, 138
Political Parties. *See* Democratic Party, Republican Party, Green Party, Libertarian Party, Whig Party, Progressive Party
Prisons
    For-Profit Prisons, 63, 64, 67
    Prison System, 9, 11
Progressive Party, 16
Public, Jane Q., 101, 102, 103, 117, 118, 119, 120
Reagan, Ronald, 14, 16
Republican Party, 6, 7, 8, 12, 13, 14, 15, 16, 18, 19, 20, 22, 27, 35, 36, 38, 51, 52, 57, 61, 63, 76, 77, 78, 79, 80, 83, 84, 85, 87, 89, 94, 95, 96, 97, 107, 108, 113, 116, 118, 119, 120, 125, 130, 132, 135
Revenue Act of 1861, 6
Revenue Act of 1862, 7
Rhode Island, 9, 19, 31, 40, 107, 108, 110, 119, 121, 127, 131
Sanders, Bernie, 20, 52, 96
Scholastic Aptitude Test (SAT), 59, 60
    Evidence-Based Reading, Writing, 59
Slavery, 9, 10
South Carolina, 9, 20, 40, 107, 108, 110, 119, 121, 127, 131
South Dakota, 9, 20, 40, 107, 108, 110, 119, 121, 127, 131
Swift, Taylor, 124, 125, 126, 128
Taxation, 7, 8, 14, 15, 25, 28, 32, 41, 75
Tennessee, 9, 20, 40, 107, 108, 110, 119, 121, 127, 131
Texas, 9, 10, 11, 19, 40, 44, 45, 46, 47, 48, 76, 78, 107, 108, 110, 119, 121, 127, 131

Third Party, 18, 93, 94, 97, 103, 105, 106, 109, 112, 115, 116, 120, 122, 125, 126, 128, 129, 130, 132, 138
TikTok, 2, 3, 87, 90
Trump, Donald, 8, 14, 20, 52, 106, 108, 109, 114, 117, 118, 124, 125, 126, 127, 128, 130, 134, 138
United States Census Bureau, 28
Utah, 9, 20, 40, 107, 108, 110, 119, 121, 127, 131
Vermont, 9, 19, 20, 31, 40, 44, 107, 108, 110, 119, 121, 127, 131
Veterans, 7, 12, 150, 157
Virginia, 9, 19, 40, 106, 107, 108, 110, 119, 121, 127, 131, 138
Washington (District of Columbia), 105
Washington (State), 9, 19, 35, 40, 77, 105, 107, 108, 110, 119, 121, 127, 131
Washington Post, 35
West Virginia, 9, 40, 107, 108, 110, 119, 121, 127, 131
Whig Party, 94, 95
Wisconsin, 9, 19, 40, 87, 106, 107, 108, 110, 118, 119, 121, 127, 130, 131
Wyoming, 9, 20, 40, 107, 108, 110, 119, 121, 127, 131

About the Author

Nick Powers is an independent researcher, author, painter, board game designer, content creator, and roller coaster enthusiast. You might find him at your neighborhood theme park, riding roller coasters. His other works include:

As the Pizza Burns — a novel about customer service workers.

Eclipse: A Nick Powers Game — a two-player competitive strategy game.

F*ck it, Let's Paint! — an upcoming Amazon Prime Original painting show.

Follow online at all platforms:
@ThatNickPowersGuy

Milton Keynes UK
Ingram Content Group UK Ltd.
UKHW020744051024
449151UK00011B/414

Hold up!

It's an election year, and there are a few things I guarantee you've never seen before.

If you've ever wanted to know how to get a third party elected, where big money in politics comes from, how rigged our system is, and especially how to fix it, this book is for you.

Yes, you. Not your college professor, congressperson, or crazy uncle who you avoid during holidays — it was written for you.

You've always wanted to change the world, right?

In Quick! Before You Vote… I answer questions in the same familiar dialogue as you've seen in short-form content. I take a talking point, dissect it, and show unbiased results. If you want to learn more about the world, especially if your goal is to save it, let's do it together. Right here. Right now.

But do it quickly… before you vote!